Poems Written Abroad

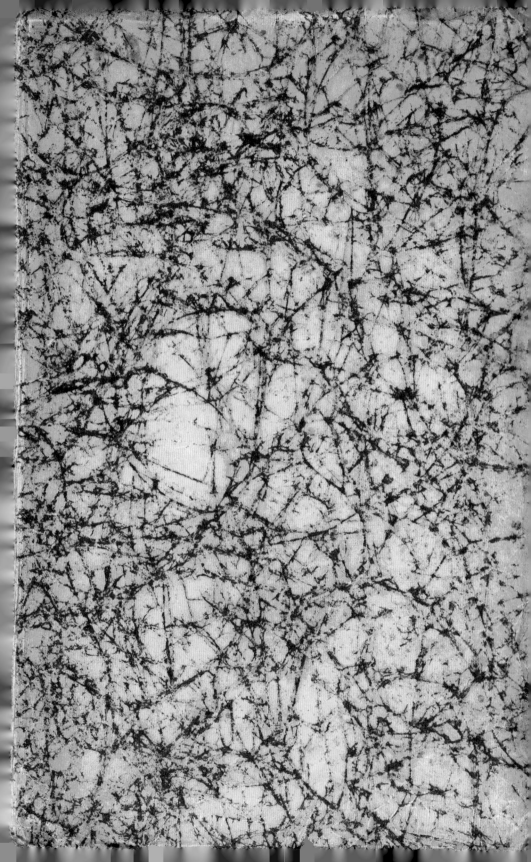

SPECIAL PUBLICATIONS OF THE LILLY LIBRARY
Indiana University Press in collaboration with the Lilly Library

Frankenstein 200: The Birth, Life, and Resurrection of Mary Shelley's Monster
Rebecca Baumann, foreword by Jonathan Kearns

Poems Written Abroad

THE LILLY LIBRARY MANUSCRIPT

Stephen Spender

EDITED BY
Christoph Irmscher

This book is a publication of

Indiana University Press
Office of Scholarly Publishing
Herman B Wells Library 350
1320 East 10th Street
Bloomington, Indiana 47405 USA

iupress.indiana.edu

Manufactured in the United States of America

Library of Congress Cataloging-in-Publication Data

Names: Spender, Stephen, 1909-1995, author. | Irmscher, Christoph,
    editor. | Lilly Library (Indiana University, Bloomington)
Title: Poems written abroad : the Lilly Library manuscript /
    Stephen Spender ; edited by Christoph Irmscher.
Description: Bloomington, Indiana : Indiana University Press, [2019] | Series: Special
    publications of the Lilly Library | Includes bibliographical references.
Identifiers: LCCN 2018052144 (print) | LCCN 2018056940 (ebook) | ISBN
    9780253041692 (e-book) | ISBN 9780253041678 (cloth : alk. paper)
Subjects: LCSH: Spender, Stephen, 1909-1995—Manuscripts—Facsimiles. |
    Manuscripts, English—Indiana—Bloomington—Facsimiles.
Classification: LCC PR6037.P47 (ebook) | LCC PR6037.
    P47 A6 2019 (print) | DDC 821/.912—dc23
LC record available at https://lccn.loc.gov/2018052144

1 2 3 4 5   24 23 22 21 20 19

The editor would like to dedicate this volume
to Matt Spender
in appreciation of his generosity and support

CONTENTS

ABBREVIATIONS

Works by Stephen Spender

BC   *The Burning Cactus.* 1936. The Faber Library. London: Faber and
        Faber, 1941.

CP   *Collected Poems 1928–1953.* New York: Random, 1955.

D   *Dolphins.* New York: St. Martin's Press, 1994.

J   *Journals 1939–1983.* Ed. John Goldsmith. New York: Random, 1986.

MP   "Miss Pangborne." Unpublished typescript. Spender Ms. 328.
        Bodleian Library, Oxford University.

NSJ   *New Selected Journals 1939–1995.* Ed. Lara Feigel and John
        Sutherland, with Natasha Spender. London: Faber and Faber, 2012.

NCP   *New Collected Poems.* Ed. Michael Brett. London: Faber and Faber,
        2004.

T   *The Temple: A Novel.* New York: Grove, 1988.

WWW   *World within World: The Autobiography of Stephen Spender.* 1951.
        Introduction by John Bayley. New York: Modern Library, 2001.

ACKNOWLEDGMENTS

This edition would not have been possible without the help of many dedicated people. First and foremost, I would like to thank Matthew and Lizzie Spender, who gave me permission to edit and publish the manuscript. Matt has provided unstinting support and encouragement throughout the long gestation of this manuscript, and I want to acknowledge his infinite patience and unrelenting generosity. This edition is dedicated to him.

I was delighted that the estate of Stephen Spender approved of my plan to edit this book, and I want give particular thanks to Jessica West of Ed Victor Ltd. for confirming my sense that the early Spender is fascinating. Peer-Olaf Richter allowed us to use a wonderful portrait of young Spender from the collection of his friend Herbert List for the dust jacket of the book.

Zachary Downey of the Lilly Library took the photographs of Spender's manuscript that form the core of this volume. I also want to salute the efforts of Mallory Cohn, who, as her final project for one of my archival studies classes, produced a first annotated transcription of Spender's text. Her unerring critical sense has guided my own work. Colin Harris at the Bodleian Library helped me identify and obtain a much-needed source from Spender's papers.

My profound thanks for various acts of kindness and assistance go to the faculty and staff of the Lilly Library, including its Director, Joel Silver; the former Curator of Manuscripts, Cherry Williams, as well the current Curator, Erika Dowell; former Reference Librarian, David Frasier; and Head of Public Services, Rebecca Baumann. Cherry Williams initiated the contact with Indiana University Press, where Gary Dunham, Peggy Solic, Tony Brewer, and my editor *extraordinaire* Anna Francis worked on making the final product a reality. I owe thanks also to Ava Dickerson, Anna Arays, and Nathan Schmidt for their proofreading efforts. Finally, my immense gratitude for the counsel given by Professor Massimo Bacigalupo, who reviewed an earlier version of this edition and offered advice on the final draft, and, last but certainly not least, for the unwavering friendship and continuing inspiration of Breon Mitchell.

BLOOMINGTON, AUGUST 2018
Christoph Irmscher

INTRODUCTION

Poems written in early youth and poems written in old age have one thing in common. Their value is usually determined in relation to something they're not—the masterworks of middle age, composed at the height of one's powers. But if a poet's late work is usually seen as a kind of summation, a gathering of forces, bathed in the light of the wisdom accumulated during a lifetime, poems written early in a poet's career are cursed by what they aren't yet. Granted, occasionally a young writer bursts on to the scene with work so extraordinary, so finished, that he or she challenges such orthodoxies. Arthur Rimbaud, "heaven-born boy with a Hellfire tongue," as Stephen Spender almost reverently addressed him in a late poem, is a case in point. But young Stephen Spender was no Rimbaud (or "Rimb," as he addressed him in that poem).[1] And therein lies, precisely, the appeal of the present volume.

Poems Written Abroad is a slim, unpublished manuscript compiled by eighteen-year-old Stephen Spender during a three-month summer vacation in 1927 in France and Switzerland. He wrote his poems in a blank, octavo-sized notebook of thirty-six leaves with batik covers that he had purchased while in France.[2] He numbered the pages, added a dedication, and drew an elaborate cover illustration. Most of the poems show little or no revision, which suggests that they were fair copies from drafts written down elsewhere. In other words, *Poems Written Abroad* was not a casual affair. This was not the last time, incidentally, that Spender used a special notebook for his poetry. The Lilly Library owns two notebooks with fancily ornamented covers containing Spender's drafts for *Ruins and Visions* (dated 1939–1941; see fig. 0.1). The aesthetic aspects of bookmaking had appealed to him early on. In 1926, for example, he gathered several pamphlets of poetry, by authors as diverse as Laurence Binyon and Walt Whitman, into a nineteenth-century half-calf binding, which he proudly inscribed, inside the front cover: "bound by me in 1926—Stephen Spender." Two years later, he used a hand press he had acquired to typeset a small collection of his own poems, *Nine Experiments*, as well as his new friend W. H. Auden's first collection of poems.[3]

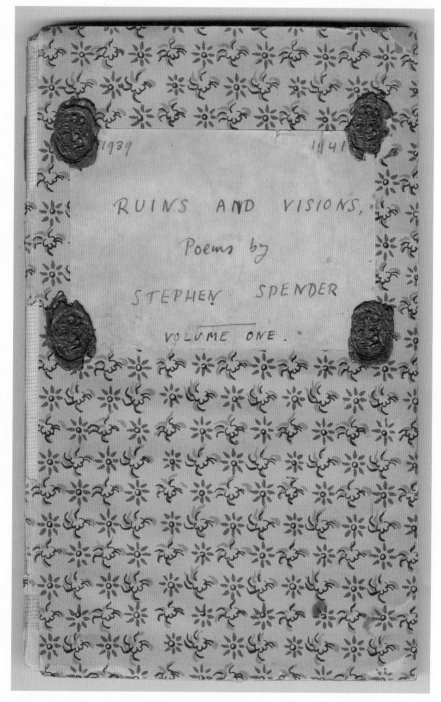

Figure 0.1. Stephen Spender, draft notebook for *Ruins and Visions*, vol. 1. 1939–1941. The Lilly Library.

How and why Spender lost track of *Poems Written Abroad*, a work in which he had invested so much time and care, remains a mystery. Sometime before 1956, John Negley Yarnall, a professor of English at Wilson College in Chambersburg, Pennsylvania, and a collector of manuscripts and rare books, purchased the autograph, along with manuscripts by W. H. Auden and Virginia Woolf, from David Randall, who then headed the rare books department at Scribner's in New York.[4] When Randall became the first director of the newly created Lilly Library at Indiana University, he was looking to build a "representative collection" of manuscripts by modern writers, and he got back in touch with Yarnall, now a Professor of English at Montgomery College in Maryland. Yarnall agreed to sell his Spender, Woolf, and Auden autographs back to Randall, for a total of $2,500.[5] It appears that Yarnall had, at some point, considered editing at least the Spender poems for publication and had even written to Spender himself to get his permission.

Yarnall provided Randall with the originals of his correspondence with Spender. They tell a somewhat comical story. It seems Spender at first drew a blank when asked about *Poems Written Abroad*.[6] But when Yarnall sought him out, after a lecture Spender had given at Georgetown University, he finally remembered and asked to see the manuscript. Yarnall obliged and dispatched it to Northwestern University, where Spender was teaching at the time. And that, for a while, was the last thing he heard. Spender had misplaced the poems without even taking a look; he probably thought they were just another one of those manuscripts that friends and strangers alike would mail him for inspection and approval: "I get sent things to read all the time." Eventually, much to Yarnall's relief, they turned up again and Spender found them to be not as "bad as he had feared."[7] Yarnall got the green light.

And, indeed, bad they are not. *Poems Written Abroad* provides us with a unique window onto an important summer in the life of one of the most important British poets of the twentieth century. In "Tradition and the Individual Talent," an essay written when Spender was just ten years old, T. S. Eliot claimed that the mind of a poet was like the shred of platinum that acts as a catalyst in a chemical reaction, bringing together the old and the new and thus vanishing in the process.[8] That is not how things worked for Stephen Spender or, I would suggest, for any poet of significance. Spender's presence—that of the adolescent Stephen as well as that of the person and poet he was to become—is felt on every page of this manuscript, as are the forces of tradition he grapples with, from Milton and Shakespeare to Rimbaud and T. S. Eliot. And so, too, are the beginnings of the unique Spenderian voice, a mix of pose, erudition, and, at times, a kind of honesty so disarming that it turns into another pose.

Born on February 28, 1909, in Kensington into a literary and artistic family, Stephen Harold Spender (fig. 0.2) had, from the beginning of his life, opportunities others would dream about. His father, Harold Spender, was a journalist and Liberal politician. His formidable uncle, J. A. Spender, edited the *Westminster Gazette*, while his grandmother, Lillian Spender, had been a prolific novelist, author of such books as *Jocelyn's Mistake* and *Mark Eylmer's Revenge*. Not to be outdone, Harold tried his hand at novel writing too, with mixed success: "He searched neither for startling originality of plot nor hair-raising adventures," observed one reviewer about Harold's *One Man Returns* (1913), while the *Spectator* pointed out that the parents Mr. Spender had introduced as characters in the first chapters of *Call of the Siren* (1914) were disappointingly forgotten later in the book "by the author and their own children."[9] Meanwhile, Violet, Harold's wife and Stephen's mother, painted and wrote poetry ranging from lugubrious reflections on the war that had taken her brother's life to a mock obituary for her cook, the full irony of which probably wasn't clear to her: "She cooked the food for persons nine, / As well as friends who came to dine, / All wanting special little dishes."[10] Art ran in the family, if ever so feebly, and people were vaguely cosmopolitan. Violet's parents, Ernest and Hilda Schuster, brought a combined tradition of German culture and Judaism into the family that certainly helped shape Spender's own worldliness. In "The Ambitious Son," a poem from *Ruins and Visions* (1942), Spender recalled a childhood overshadowed by the feeling that he was failing to live up to the family name. "My childhood went for rides on your wishes," he told his father, now long dead:

> As a beggar's eye strides a tinsel horse,
> And how I reeled before your windy lashes
> Fit to drive a paper boat off its course!
>
> Deep in my heart I learned this lesson
> As well have never been born at all
> As live through life and fail to impress on
> Time, our family name, inch-tall.

The bitter irony palpable in that last line wasn't available to Stephen when he was a child. As an adult, he remembers his childhood as dominated by the feeling of being lost "in a vast, deserted garden." But although he had learned to see his father's

Facing, Figure 0.2. Stephen Spender, 1929. Unknown photographer. The Lilly Library.

goals for what they really were, he had continued to live his life as if he still wanted to please him: "O Father, to a grave of fame I faithfully follow!"[11]

Stephen's mother, Violet, died when he was only ten, and Harold, discouraged by his lack of measurable political success, did not survive an operation on his spleen in 1926, accepting even before he went under the knife that he would die. In his autobiography, Stephen spoke of his own weakness, the lack of a "strong will," as the curse of his life and the limitation that prevented him from achieving true greatness as a poet. But he also claimed that laziness was a way to rebel against his family and their emphasis on morality, work, and discipline. Young Stephen was an intense child, visited by nightmares and desires that overwhelmed him. His vivid imagination forced him to picture Christ fastened to the cross by ropes, because the thought of nails driven through his flesh was intolerable. In his autobiography, he likens his first experience of sexual pleasure, felt when wrestling with another boy, to a "sensation like the taste of a strong sweet honey . . . spreading wave upon wave, throughout my whole body." The main fear his family had implanted in him was that of becoming a "moral outcast," the fear that there might be residing in him some "final wickedness. . . , some unspeakable shame of ultimate depravity." Yet, instead of resisting wickedness, he embraced it, a risky undertaking at a time when homosexuality was still considered a crime in England. But that would be entirely too easy a reading, as Spender himself recognized. In his autobiography, Spender called himself a "wanderer," not a pilgrim—an acknowledgment that he was never quite sure what he was looking for.[12]

Many of the complexities of Stephen's childhood and adolescence are memorably captured in a novel he drafted late in life, *Miss Pangborne*,[13] a roman à clef told from the perspective of the nanny who was brought in to look after the orphaned Spender children and whose name, in real life, was Winifred Paine. As one biographer described her, Winifred became "a sort of Mary Poppins" to the Spender siblings and went on to cause a great deal of confusion to the adolescent Stephen.[14] He appears in the novel as Martin Banner, a sensitive, artistically inclined youngster deeply interested in the sculptures of Jacob Epstein and the paintings of Augustus John, a passion considered immoral by his inefficient father "because of the nudes."[15]

When she arrives, Miss Caroline Pangborne finds the Banner household in disarray and Martin/Stephen in mental distress, deeply affected by the fall of a previous live-in nanny, Susan Sled, from their house's fourth floor. It appeared that Susan had become rather too attached to Martin's father; luckily, she survived her impulsive window tumble.[16] Right after, the traumatized Martin was sent to live for a while with his aloof grandmother, Mrs. Schelling (Hilda Schuster in real life), accompanying her to Quaker meetings, where she would invariably fall asleep. Mrs. Schelling tried to implant in Martin a fear of the consequences of sex (venereal disease) and a respect for class boundaries especially when it came to marriage. The novel draft also recounts a feverish dream in which Martin, carted off to the hospital for treatment of scarlet fever, sees himself floating above foggy London, high above the honking cars, roaring lorries, and pealing church bells until he finds himself entering a corridor of flames lined by Blakean figures, at the end of which he glimpsed the Light that was God. Or so he dreamed until he awoke, cured of his fever.[17]

The novel remains firmly anchored in Miss Pangborne's consciousness, and it is through her eyes that we see Martin/Stephen, a remarkable feat of authorial self-detachment. Tall, angular, stooping slightly, Martin looks awkward, like a crane out of his element. His handshake is too soft, and he seems permanently distracted. His older brother Adam (i.e., Michael Spender) mercilessly mocks him for wearing an ill-fitting suit with vertical stripes that only emphasized his "verticality." But despite his evident shyness, Martin/Stephen knows how to make an entrance. Not the "willowy aesthetic type," he appears more genuinely talented than his brother Adam/Michael, who plays Beethoven sonatas as one would slice a cucumber.[18]

Art, for Martin, is sacred. He is troubled by Miss Pangborne's account of a sister whose mental economy hinged on her not forgetting to take her thyroid pills, a threat to his naïve belief that "intelligence—wisdom—imagination—in a person were or should be—independent of the condition of his or of her glands." As Martin/Stephen sees it, the world fashioned by the creative imagination of a Shakespeare "was a supreme and somehow self-sustaining world of truth." How horrible to imagine a "slight deficiency of some secretion of the glands might extinguish in the minds of the living that whole world of Shakespeare and Beethoven —like a turned off tap." The male body, with its furtive needs and unexplained desires, is a mystery to Martin, but an enticing one, as becomes evident in the erotically charged account of a Dartmoor walking tour, during which, by endless questioning, he coaxes a friend into masturbating in front of him. The trip ends, as it in fact did in Stephen Spender's life, when he gets news of his father's death.[19]

Looking back from the distance of several decades at his younger self, Stephen Spender captures precisely the way an adolescent poet's overactive mind works, fusing his environment into sharply contoured, often outrageous images that are as much the product of his reading as they are of direct observation. Take Martin's/Stephen's response to the ocean he sees on that Dartmoor hiking trip: to him, it is "an empty stage set waiting for the entrance of some virtuoso soloist."

And, lo and behold, a minute later that soloist arrives: a fishing boat, "its bows thrusting through the water quite slowly. The chugging of its engine within the enclosing emptiness made it seem like a solo instrument with the surrounding bay its sounding board."[20] That soloist, of course, is none other than a metaphor for Martin/Stephen himself. The image self-consciously celebrates his wished-for emergence as a poet, which takes place, fittingly, just as he is about to find out that his father has died. In "Variations on My Life," published in *The Still Centre* (1939), Spender offered a poignant reflection on his struggle to be at least modestly authentic in his writing. As if to mock his penchant for pat phrases and derivative images, he called himself a "sociable puppet painted with a mouth," The task was, he went on, to "look down" on his life and "see a life," to give to that puppet's mouth "a voice / That is not death / But its own truth."[21]

When Winifred Paine, the real-life model for the fictional Miss Pangborne, entered the Spender household on October 4, 1926, Stephen was already quite the poet, at least in his own estimation. In December 1925, as he was attending University College School in London, the school's literary magazine published his poem titled "Procrastination," made memorable by the line, "I will work to-morrow."[22] In March the following year, *The Beanstalk* ran his sonnet on spring: "O month of blossoming plum, and dazzling pear / O later season when the may-flower throws."[23] Stephen's paean to spring was part of a longer sequence of sonnets. In letters to a woman named Sylvia Crum, whom he much later identified as a nanny who had been unhappily in love with his father, Stephen self-deprecatingly commented on these early efforts.[24] Was Sylvia Crum the inspiration for "Susan Sled," the lovelorn governess in *Miss Pangborne* who had hurled herself out of the window? Spirited, modern, and a little overweight, Susan had the effect, "through the considerable charm of her vivacity," of making Hubert Banner/Harold Spender "accept opinions from her which he would not have tolerated from anyone else." She was also literate: in Spender's manuscript she is described as a student of English literature at London University originally from Bath. If she was Hubert/Harold's lover, to Martin/Stephen she was not a nanny but a friend and confidante with whom he would regularly discuss his favorite writers, Thomas Hardy, Arnold Bennett, and the Georgian poets.[25]

The letters that Stephen addressed to Sylvia were written after her departure from the Spender residence. Stephen's tone is cheerful, cocky, even flirtatious, as if now that Sylvia was no longer living with them he could take his father's place in her favor. "I must not write about the Spring," Stephen intoned in yet another adolescent spring poem, which he repeated for Sylvia's benefit before he had even begun his letter. "It would be *such* a hackneyed thing." But then he also confidently included with his letter a copy of *The Beanstalk* which contained, precisely, the spring sonnet he had already published. He signed the letter with "Much Love."[26] In a subsequent letter, he confessed that he had spent much time reading Rupert Brooke, the idealistic, golden-haired war sonneteer, who, as Stephen might have realized, even looked a bit like him. Brooke's influence can indeed be felt in some of the worst lines Stephen repeats for Sylvia: "Dost thou remember how on one far height / We saw surmount the Plain an army hut / Cursing the land, and so knew Mars a slut?"[27] But in another installment of his sonnet cycle he quotes in the same letter, sonnet "X," a preview of one of the themes pursued in *Poems Written Abroad*, Stephen brilliantly ironizes his own reaching after poetic fame. He describes what happens when one mistakes the mere promise of future glory for actual accomplishment:

> O I shall write great poems & books one day!
> > Broad-metred epics flowing slow & strong,
> > Stately as rivers; many a noble play;
> > And prose relieved with rippling lyric song.
> > Posterity will learn my awe-some name
> > Coupled with Shakespeare; schoolboys will be told
> > With threats to learn my lines. (Therein lies fame!)
> > Oh I shall do great things 'ere I am old!
> My eyes scan early that far-off bird
> > Futurity; I hear its flattering song;
> > Content, drop pen, & let it fill my head.
> Soon I will write. . . . Yet dreaming once, I feared
> > That when I'd listened to it very long,
> > One morrow, listening still, that I was dead.

The sycophantic bird "Futurity" whose intoxicating song prevents the self-enamored poet from tackling the serious business of actually writing the "rippling lyric song[s]" for which he expects to be famous is an inspired invention. Even better is the prediction that schoolboys will have to be threatened to memorize Spenderian lines, a vision that severely qualifies the poet's dreams of prospective awesomeness.

As if dismayed by this detour into comedy, the next sonnet quoted by Stephen presents a more tragic version of the same theme: "Thou wilt do mighty things ere thou art old," the poem begins, a promise thoroughly deflated by the final tercet:

> Soon I will shall [*sic*] write. . . . Two dreams ago I heard
> An angel say, "when thou hast listened long
>   One morrow, listening still thou wilt be dead!"

Reminding Sylvia that this is mere poetic posturing, Stephen closes his letter by pointing out that he is, after all, only seventeen years old; he is, he says, excited about his upcoming walking tour with his friend John Cornforth—the same hike described so memorably in *Miss Pangborne*, cut short when he learned that his father had died.

Harold Spender, Stephen's ineffective father, was laid to rest, "a crumpled clown," in April 1926.[28] Nanny Winifred, half French, an inveterate cigarette smoker fond of cars and equipped with outspoken views on sex, filled whatever indistinct void the dead Harold had left, and the newly orphaned Spender children fell in love with her. Having won admission to University College Oxford, Stephen was, at his own request, sent to Nantes in France to acquire facility in a foreign language. Living in a dull pastor's joyless household, he was desperately unhappy, his loneliness interrupted only briefly when one of Winifred's letters arrived. During meals, the pastor would sit across from him, "tears streaming from his sore, red eyes," since he suffered from hay fever. Stephen's walks through the dusty, hot French countryside brought little relief, except for the fantasies in which he indulged as he was walking. A particularly memorable one involved a man approaching him and asking that he sleep with his wife "behind this hedgerow," since the man was infertile and could not give her a child. In the classes he attended at the Lycée Clemenceau, the boys around him swapped newspaper clippings that dealt with women's health; the sheer mention of female body parts got them worked up. Stephen communicated his unhappiness in his letters home, until his wish was granted and he was, at Winifred's recommendation, sent on to Lausanne. There, in a *pensionnat* overlooking the shores of Lake Geneva, he fell somewhat unhappily in love with a fellow boarder from England, David Mclean.[29]

This attempted affair was the subject of Stephen's first attempt at writing a novel or novella, which he was planning to call "Torso." An excerpt from this manuscript was later published, in revised form, as "By the Lake."[30] Here Stephen appears as "Richard Birney," a nervous young boy perennially short of money who blames his attraction to men on having been deprived by his upbringing of any serious knowledge of sex. "The result of neglecting children and never telling them anything about sex is that they often get to know in a wrong way about it."[31]

His would-be boyfriend is called "Donauld"—just the right kind of name to stir Richard's desires, which are already fired up by his constant immersion in poetry. Wandering into Richard's room, Donauld picks up one of his productions and makes fun of it, reading it slowly and stopping at the end of each line to chuckle at the amateurishness of such lines as "*Since I had loved ambition; since the stars / Had seemed most near, and my Olympian friends / The gods to whom the sun its glory lends,*" and so forth. Richard is embarrassed. "With an immediate and unaccustomed critical perception he saw how impudent he had been to write 'gods,' 'stars' and 'sun.'" Richard blushed. "Bloody rot," that poetry thing, opines Donauld. What good does it do anyone?[32]

What indeed? Richard refers Donauld to Shakespeare's sonnet 71, the perfect text for his situation, as it expresses, in most naked form, the "pathos of the un-loved speaker" (in Helen Vendler's phrase): "No longer mourn for me when I am dead / Than you shall hear the sullen, surly bell / Give warning to the world that I am fled." See, Richard triumphantly concludes, "poetry does mean something sometimes." But Donauld prefers the impersonal comforts offered by his religion to such expressions of private anguish: "I'm going to convert you one day."[33]

News of Winifred's serious illness and of an operation she might have to undergo nipped the would-be affair between Stephen and David Maclean in the bud and hastened Stephen's return home. As soon as he was back, however, Win-ifred made a miraculous recovery. What transpired between Stephen and her we'll never know; Winifred burned all the letters he had sent her from France and Switzerland. *Poems Written Abroad* thus remains as the most significant testimony to these formative months in Spender's life.[34]

One striking feature of the little volume is the generous amount of unused paper. The individual poems appear, with the exception of a draft stanza for "The Boy Who Was Called 'The Nightingale,'" only *recto*. In his correspondence with David Randall, the manuscript's last owner, John Yarnall, claimed that Spender had intended the volume for an unnamed traveling companion, who was to add poems of his own. That might indeed explain the blank space. But there is no evidence of such a companion anywhere, and while Spender often hid the details and the exact nature of his relationships, he usually at least admitted that they had taken place.[35] A more likely explanation for the empty pages is that Spender, who was deeply invested in the aesthetic appearance of the volume, worried his ink might bleed through the paper.

The poems are arranged chronologically, beginning on May 1 and ending with a series of poems written on July 27, 1927, with breaks occurring between June 1 and 12 and then again between June 30 and July 14, periods during which Stephen may have traveled. In addition, the first seven poems are introduced by short, stylized prose inserts that set the scene, in a tone reminiscent of Baudelaire's prose poems in *Le Spleen de Paris* (1869). Clearly, Spender thought of *Poems Written Abroad* as a kind of book from the beginning—hence the elaborate sketch he drew as a cover image. It is a self-portrait of sorts: wearing a jaunty cap, Stephen sits under an umbrella in what might be a café in France or Switzerland. His long legs are poking out awkwardly from under the round table, and a pile of books sits before him. An abstractly drawn sun illuminates—and a crudely rendered angel appears to bless—the picturesque landscape and the small lake, adorned with a small sailboat, drawn behind Stephen's right shoulder as well as the medieval town, pressed against the side of a mountain, behind his left. Two couples are dancing or hugging on a square. By way of contrast, in the lower right corner, naked bodies can be seen writhing in a roughly rendered representation of hell. So that there's no doubt, the French word "ENFERS"—a nod to both the Christian hell and Arthur Rimbaud's hallucinatory underworld of the soul—wraps itself through this vignette. Bellows in hand, a devil makes sure that the fire does not go out.[36]

Spender has drawn himself with his back to both heaven and hell, in a pensive attitude. The little sketch almost programmatically summarizes his situation during his enforced stay abroad—longing for an experience of the sublime, he felt himself constantly pulled into the cesspools of sin, into the illicit world of physical pleasure that he did not understand. In one of the later poems in the collection, "The Ballad of Money," remembering the ethereally blue waters of Lake Geneva, he evokes his spirit's longing "to burst away from flesh, & have a poet's eye," a desire made more complicated in a world where everyone worships at the altar of instant sensual gratification.

For all its overt stylishness, *Poems Written Abroad* is deeply autobiographical. Among the poems written in Lausanne is a sonnet explicitly addressed to Winifred Paine. "To W. E. P." qualifies as one of the more stilted contributions in the entire sequence, perhaps because Spender wasn't sure about how to properly contain the complicated emotions caused by the news that the woman who was so much more than a governess to him was ill. Describing her affliction, unpersuasively, as a kind of weather event—the disappearing sun darkens the mountains while the river freezes over—Spender imagines himself as a light-deprived summer field of grain, waiting eagerly for her blessing or, more specifically, the news that she is well again. The consciously archaic language ("thou," the use of "gloom" as a verb, the less-than-original imagery) filters and distances the occasion for the poem, as if the "glooming" mentioned in the first line had already been too personal an admission. "Consolation of Dust," the poem that immediately follows (and the last poem proper in the collection) expresses, in weepy detail, the extent of the speaker's love for an unspecified "you," which the poet imagines as so vast that he thinks of his lover in terms of hemispheres ("Thy body the dark East, thy soul the West"). By contrast, the poet himself is the dust under his lover's feet—but not in the sense that Whitman once imagined himself, life-affirmingly, as the grass that grows under the reader's boot soles. Here as elsewhere in the collection, as one would expect in a poet so young, Stephen's emotions, deeply but dimly felt, exceed his poetic capabilities.

Almost every poem in his collection reflects Spender's worry that, although he wants to be and indeed feels he *must* be a poet, the world around him has not been waiting for him to be made into a poem. If Eliot's *The Waste Land* had returned poetry to the schoolroom, Spender was a reluctant student, still hankering for the fragments of the tradition Eliot had shattered. Incidentally, that feeling stayed with him throughout his career: "What do I speak but dead men's words? What are my thoughts but dead men's minds?"[37] In *Love-Hate Relations* (1974), a study of shared themes and sensibilities in English and American literature, Spender would later describe the dilemma of the Georgian poet in terms that well describe the situation in which he found himself in 1927: "The young English poet's sense of his vocation went with the realization that he would have to acquire skill in writing poems in the form and manner in which they had already been written." Through mastery of the Petrarchan sonnet or the Spenserean stanza, the young poet thought he would "obtain freedom to exercise his instinct, like a bird learning to fly." It did not occur to this poet that the old forms might no longer fit the demands of modern life.[38]

At the outset of Spender's career, form indeed provided a temporary refuge. In the opening poem of the collection ("Sonnet on Absence"), Spender shows off his early command of the Petrarchan sonnet, but he does so with at least some degree of irony. The smirking, smug-tongued host in the poem, bringing wine and toast to the impressionable speaker, a reincarnation in different form of Eliot's sinister, greasily seductive merchant from Smyrna in *The Waste Land*, was based on the bleary-eyed pastor with whom Stephen had been placed in Nantes. Unresponsive to the man's advances, Spender remains focused on the "you" back home, likely Winifred, whom he represents symbolically through a lone tree in the wasteland, a tree "pensively still, fair, kind, and queenly-graced," which can do what the speaker cannot: make the landscape beautiful again. Spender's poem is a sonnet "on absence" in more than one way. It evokes the absent "you" but also the absence of the poet—as the beautifier of his environment—from his home country as well as, in a way, from his own poetry. Spender gives us not an image of the tree-as-poem (condemned to cliché status by Joyce Kilmer's "I think I shall never see / A poem lovely as a tree") but the tree-as-poet.[39] The smile of the last line seems oddly detached grammatically from the rest of the poem, but it's a fitting characterization of the speaker's own separation from his environment.

"The Chateau Garden," written in rhymed couplets, continues the characterization of the poet as non-participant observer. Disenchanted with present-day Nantes, he lingers, sketch pad in hand, in the garden of the large Château des ducs de Bretagne and dreamily imagines a past which, however, turns out to be as tear-filled as the poet's existence today. The richly dressed ladies and elders are crying, outwardly or inwardly, while they go about their business. In this world, the poets and dandies do not enjoy a wider view either: "And there are artists poets & dandies / whose narrow wit their only stand is." The rhyme "dandies / stand is" is so awkward that one must assume that it was intended to be that way—as were, one hopes, the "rose bushes" put to shame by the ladies' "blushes." By the ending of the poem, afraid that he might be swallowed up by the imagined scene and become part of what he has just been watching, the poet flees. The result of his time travel is devastating: while he is at odds with the present, there is no place for him in that world either, as his outfit emphasizes. Among those unhappy spirits of the past he would be a "trousered ghost," an image reminiscent perhaps of Eliot's repressed Prufrock, who was so determined to wear the "bottoms" of his trousers rolled. Prufrock famously saw "the women come and go / Talking of Michelangelo," a line Spender likely remembered when he had his poet say, "So now two hundred years ago / I sit and watch the ladies go." The creative blending of immediate poetic present and remote medieval past captures the speaker's strangeness.

For the young poet, the weight of the past, precisely because he knows he has no place in it, is overwhelming, and awareness of all the poets that have preceded him paralyzes his efforts, as Spender admits in a poem blandly titled "Stanzas." One need only think of the powerful father figure in Sylvia Plath's "The Colossus" (1959), a bitter comment on the maintenance work the poet has to perform on the crumbling ruins of the past. Spender lacks Plath's sarcasm—for him, the fact that the earth is old casts doubt on whether he will be able to transform it into something that it is not. Nature, in this poem, is cold, hard-crusted, frosty. This isn't Spender pretending to be older than his years; this is the young poet despairing that there is little left for him to do other than to shout "belated truth." Everything has already been written about, by poets stronger than him. In Spender's world, the lyre, that ancient instrument of the aspiring poet, is just that: ancient, worn-out. Even if "divinelier strung / Than Virgil's," it cannot but celebrate the "old exploréd sweets:— / The sky, the trees; and blossom, like a poem from each branch rung." The earth is sick of the poems that have been written about it; any truth that we might still coax from it must be a hopelessly belated one. Spender's poem revels in its own derivativeness—a kind of wintry version of Keats's "To Autumn." Wearing its ironic attitude to life on its poetic sleeve, the poem exhausts itself in its own self-declared ingenuity.

In "To a Poet," Spender tries to turn such belatedness into an asset, relinquishing himself to another, stronger, older, and therefore "maturer" poet, someone more "more deft than I," who knows how to get some tunes out of the fickle instrument that is the poet's heart: "more obedient be it to thy mind / Than mine (unnurtured), for it needs such might." And in "The Boy Who Was Called 'The Nightingale,'" he also considers an alternative to this strong father-figure, a seductive young boy nicknamed for his sweet voice which makes all other things around him (birds, trees, flowers) seem like mere accompaniments to his song. While this poem is a homosexual fantasy, it is also part of Spender's quest to try out roles for himself, ways in which it will still be possible for him to be a poet. Here as elsewhere in this collection, he is not averse to the occasional corniness: "The little flowers all shook, afraid, / And then, towards him in a twinkle / Leapt swiftly with bright heads that tinkle." But he uses such devices self-consciously. As the poem continues, the insistent daintiness of Spender's language switches from bothersome to mesmerizing. It's as if the poem revels in its own preciousness, each line a reminder that such cloying sweetness isn't a good option either: "O let us leave him singing there!"

Not unexpectedly in such a young but intense poet and avid reader of the French symbolists, there is also the inevitable flirtation with death as a welcome relief from the pressures of the aesthetic life, as in "Tail-piece": "How easily now a great hand might put me to sleep, / and I go on lying in this delicious melancholy for ever." Death is the poet's only friend, stipulates the "Epitaph on a Poet," a concise quatrain that appears at the very end of the manuscript and begins with a line that suggests that the eighteen-year-old author was trying out another fantasy role here: "They said my life was wild; but still I led it."[40] That Spender wasn't exactly referring to himself is reinforced by "Two Sonnets," a pair of Shakespearean sonnets in which the poet angrily rejects the insinuation, made by an unspecified source and explained in an inserted prose commentary, that he had engaged in the reading of "immodest literature with the same intent as the type of youth he dislikes cuts vulgar paragraphs out of newspapers." As a "high-aspiring" poet, he is higher on the evolutionary scale than the pimply sex addicts at the Lycée Clemenceau: "Youth sickens me when 'tis a growth I know / Corporeal, gross, and keen lust to pursue." This is the same Spender who, in a poem written a few years later, would say of himself that he'd rather "record the act of wishing" than its fulfillment: "I move hands for touching, / But am never nearer than touching."[41]

But then, in a twist that anticipates Spender's later excursions into the gay under-worlds of Berlin and Barcelona, Spender adds, as the final couplet of the second poem: "And so I'd fall, because to sin is better / Than be called sinning, doing no such matter." In other words, it's preferable actually to engage in depravity than to be merely accused of it without cause. In *Poems Written Abroad*, sinning is still something done by other people. But the warning signs are there.

For example, images of the "wild life" are vividly conjured in the longest poem in the collection, "The Confession of a Monk," in which furtive sexual longing and adolescent guilt combine. Spender's lecherous monk, unchastened by the blind-ness with which he has been stricken, assumes his rightful place beside other sensually deprived monks in poetry.[42] The form of the confession allows Spender to experiment with a longer narrative poem. It is no coincidence that "The Con-fession of a Monk" follows the sonnets dealing with charges of impropriety. Like Spender, the monk is not contrite: God has, he says, "gentler ways for less vile deeds." But unlike Spender, he has really sinned and seems to be altogether proud of what he has done. The monk confesses only to unravel, at great and salacious length, the nature of his offense, which takes place on Easter, in a pastoral setting, described in evocative visual detail (a transparent river, the banks lined with irises). As the monk revisits the mass rape that he instigated and actively took part in, his "hungry mouth" once again, in his feverish imagination, passes over over the body of a dark-eyed beauty. The end of the poem leaves no doubt that the monk's sensual proclivities have not calmed down: eager to be touched, he feels the wind caressing his flesh and the warm sun brushing his face like the wings of a bird.

A sexual predator is also at the center of the only poem from this collection Spender re-used later, when he included it in a little volume he printed private-ly the next year, on a hand press he had acquired. The model for "The Original Bluebeard" was Gilles de Rais, a medieval French nobleman and confessed killer of children who was executed and buried in Nantes, and that coincidence likely inspired Spender to write the little poem. In clipped, concentrated lines, Spender evokes Bluebeard's troubling otherness and his freakishness. His hair is blue, the color of the sky, as one could say, were it not for the fact that in France even the sky is not real, a silken artifact. The poem is all about visual cues: people do not hear Bluebeard, but when they see him, there is no doubt about his identity; "face, / And beard" give him away.

Spender has a distinct talent for creating memorable visual effects. In "She Holds a Rose," a poem giving voice to a woman clasping a rose, he creates for us an image of the woman's waxen, papery fingers getting ready to pluck the flower, "each carmine petal, stained with the late sun." And he goes all out in a poem with the complicated title "Fragment for a Possible Romance. A Description before the Storm," which seeks to describe the proverbial calmness before the storm. Comparing the sky, heavy with premonitions of the coming downpour, to a sagging piece of cloth "stretched out on four tent poles," he records how blue turns into lurid yellow, how piercingly white the dust seems, and how the rain-parched grass acquires "shiny brightness"—intense colors all, reminiscent of a Van Gogh painting. At the same time, Spender's landscapes have a curious flatness, an effect of which Spender seems fully aware, as the next stanza makes clear:

> Only the swallows dart in puzzled cubes
> with sharp black wings; and an acute-edged cry
> cuts into vague figures all the poles of sound.

Motion and sound are, as soon as they happen, transformed into shapes—cubes that appear surprised by their own existence, as it were, figures whose "vagueness" suggests that the poet, too, is not sure what is going on, except that he must follow where his imagination leads him. An unusual editorial note in the autograph tells us that the adjective "puzzled" was important to him because of the implied pun on "jag saw [jigsaw]."

A similarly surreal landscape emerges in "Clair de lune," a poem inspired by either by Verlaine or Debussy or both, which invites us to observe a mountainscape in the moonlight—likely a view Spender saw when he was in Lausanne. The memorable image of the moon spilling her milk "In silver fountains / across the mountains" prompts certain literary and cultural associations: Romeo at night wooing his Juliet and Aeneas burning with love for his Dido. They perhaps intentionally invoke a contrast that is repeated in the opposition between Mozart's music shifting around some ornamental, "fretted" leaves and the overpowering "swells" of Beethoven that "appall" the heart. (Never mind that Mozart wrote no madrigals—the m-alliteration must have been too tempting to resist.) At the end of the poem, we get a glimpse of Stravinsky dancing in the snow while "John Sebastian" Bach is rearranging stars in the sky.

But such clever modernist play ultimately doesn't satisfy. The difference between Romeo and Aeneas, between "spilt milk" and "alpenglow" is one of degree, not of kind. During his stay in Lausanne, Stephen himself had experienced "alpenglow," where the setting sun hits airborne snow or ice particles and wraps a fiery red band of light around the mountaintops. And he had written about it in "By the Lake," the prose sketch he was working on at the time, in which Richard Birney, Stephen's alter ego, goes out one night to see "the crest of mountains turned the colour of pistils in tiger lilies by the sunset." Before Richard's eyes, the alpenglow turns into an X-ray-like image of his own shortcomings: "The mountains were so clear and flat that they seemed projected on to a screen by the setting sun, and Richard felt that his own life was thrown on to a screen like that nervous and detailed picture which seemed not of rocks, but of immensely magnified skeleton leaves." This is an excellent description also of Spender's poetic dilemma in *Poems Written Abroad*, a volume thrumming with nervous excitement as it turns an unsparing lens on Stephen's inner contradictions.[43]

Spender evoked Stravinsky and Beethoven again in a poem published in 1972 and revised in 1985, "Late Stravinsky Listening to Late Beethoven." On the brink of death, weightless, "purged of every self," Stravinsky won't listen to anything but Beethoven's late quartets. As in the earlier poem, Beethoven is the epitome of authenticity, the sound from the valley that indicates a life lived to the fullest. Caught in the prison of his deafness, Beethoven turns sight into sound or, more particularly, the image of a shepherd playing a flute into the tune played by that flute or the sight of blocks of ice crashing against each other into the noise of cymbals clashing.[44] This is not synesthesia, strictly speaking, since Beethoven, from whose perspective that part of the poem is written, cannot hear but only see. Yet Spender goes on to prove that for the ultimate artist there are no limitations:

> a curve, a tune, parabola,
> Held in the eye become an ear: flies on
> Until the line at last dissolves
> Into that light where the perceiver
> Becomes one with the thing perceived,
> The hearing with the seeing. . . .

As Spender imagines him, Stravinsky, at the end of his life, can experience Beethoven's fusion of sight and sound only incompletely, by listening to a needle scratching its way through the grooves of a record. And Spender sees what Stravinsky hears. Both gesture toward the possibility of a fully authentic utterance, the fusion of hearing and seeing, which, in Spender's view, only Beethoven, the man deprived of one of his senses, experienced. In 1972, the theme of "Clair de lune" is still with Spender: unable to be fully authentic himself, he finds a measure of authenticity in noting his own lack of it or, conversely, in praising an excess of it in others, in those greater than him.[45]

If Spender is remembered for a single poem today, chances are it would be "The Truly Great," a somewhat fawning poem about precisely the class of people to which he himself knew he didn't automatically belong, "those who in their lives fought for life, / Who wore at their hearts the fire's centre."[46] Reviewing the new edition of Spender's *Collected Poems* for *The Guardian* in 2004, Ian Sansom called Spender "an awkward poet" who would redeem himself only later in life with *The Generous Days* (1971), by becoming the "Poet of Awkwardness," producing poems filled with "stumblings, hauntings, shame and confusion." But, as *Poems*

Written Abroad shows, stumblings, hauntings, shame, and confusion were Spender's themes from the beginning. He was the "Poet of Awkwardness" from the moment he put pen to paper. Yet this should not be viewed as a shortcoming or a flaw. Spender's earliest poems transcend whatever juvenile angst had motivated them. If anything, they help increase our respect for the humanity and the hard work that allowed Spender to turn himself, over many years, into at least half of the poet he wanted to be. And given who or what he wanted to be, that is no mean feat.

Poems Written Abroad thus previews the main characteristics of Spender's mature poetry: the sharp-edged images that bump against each other like the pieces of a badly made puzzle, the lavish blending of sensations, the pervasive feeling that somewhere someone is having a more authentic experience than Spender is capable of having. An entire generation of fathers has disappeared, he notes in a poem titled "1929." Refusing even to stick around as ghosts, they have left sons like him bewildered and feeling empty: "there lives no feud / Like prompting Hamlet on the castle stair." Life is a transitory matter—a brief interlude and temporary relief from isolation, until one returns to the sod, literally becoming matter again, "a stratum unreckoned by geologists, / Sod lifted, turned, slapped back again with spade."[47] Over the course of Spender's long career—he would publish his last volume, *Dolphins*, when he was eighty-five—his language eased into casualness, and unabashed autobiography (in poems about his children, grandchildren, lovers, and his fear of death) replaced the more veiled narratives of his earlier work, yet many of the concerns first expressed in *Poems Written Abroad* have remained essentially unchanged.

Cowed by those who, unlike him, are "truly great," the poet is on a constant quest for the "realer passions of the earth," for a world dazzlingly illuminated by the shine of falling snow, a world where men, in an admiring dawn, declare their love for each other, a world waiting to be "petalled" by his pen.[48] But the sense of being shut out from the living, breathing universe around him pervades his work, as if an invisible wall had been permanently placed between him and the "swarm of stars and flowers" that seemed just within his reach.[49] Thus, in "The Cries of Evening" (1933) the speaker, "town-bred" and out of place in nature, appears as the "chattering" observer being played upon like a harp by his environment, while "beasts," unconcerned, "move to their ease."[50] His parents kept him "from children who were rough / And who threw words like stones and who wore torn clothes," reflects the speaker in another poem from the early thirties, written, ironically, at a time when Spender, now under the influence of W. H. Auden and Christopher

Isherwood, actively sought out rough trade in Germany and Spain. What he was taught to fear then—"their muscles like iron / And their jerking hands and their knees tight on my arms"—he now coveted.[51] Spender's poems never contained words that hit like stones, but the clear-sightedness with which he envisions the way his poetry falls short gives his work its own cohesion, force, and dignity. "Never being, but always at the edge of Being," Spender was pursued by a sense of separateness even when he wrote love poetry, where moments of intimacy—the touch of a lover's moth-like lips, for example—are lost in the meanderings of the poet's mind, which "makes the seen / Be drowned in all that past and future / Of the once seen."[52]

Spender's experience of war only enhanced his outsider status: "I am the coward of cowards," he reflects, in one of his poems about the Spanish Civil War, which he witnessed, a journalist's pass in hand. He was at Portbou at the time, a small village at the foot of the Pyrenees, "left alone on the parapet at the exact centre," holding a newspaper in which the militiamen are not interested (they want cigarettes). Spender admires "their waving flag-like faces," in which, he thinks, "the war finds peace," a beautiful phrase that brings a touch of tenderness to their encounter. But it is a tenderness he cannot extend to himself. Shots fired at a distance penetrate him to the core, though he is, of course, not hit—a mockery of what happens to real soldiers in a war that is not, like Spender's, perceived from the sidelines. What grasps his intestines is naked fear:

> The machine-gun stitches
> My intestines with a needle, back and forth;
> The solitary, spasmodic, white puffs from the carbines
> Draw fear in white threads back and forth through my body.[53]

Here as elsewhere in Spender's poetry, the body is a vast vessel of sensations. But these are not to be trusted and are anyway best confronted when everyone else has left.[54] The price to be paid for feeling things deeply is that there's little room left for others. Alone in his house, sleepless, the poet hears a sound like "the walls / Crumbling away" and then identifies it as the voice of a friend "I shut outside / Sink or swim." And that friend ("well, he sank") is now tapping at his window: "Let me in! Let me in!" Spender's cool response: "Twenty years in the rain."[55]

It doesn't really matter who that friend is (my guess is Spender's longtime lover Tony Hyndman, who indeed "sank" after they parted). The terrifying feeling that one might miss out on the one true, authentic experience of a lifetime, the one luminous moment when everything falls into place, because one might have spent time doing the wrong things and with the wrong people, rears its ugly head everywhere Spender's poetic world. His complicated marriage to Natasha Spender—memorably described in Matthew Spender's recent book about his parents—is behind some of the most chilling lines in Spender's touching tribute to his sister-in-law, Margaret Spender, who died on Christmas Day 1945, lines addressed to his brother Humphrey: "Better in death to know / The happiness we lose / Than die in life in meaningless / Misery of those / Who lie beside chosen / Companions they never chose."[56]

Not many outside observers would have guessed the private agonies hidden under the smooth exterior of Spender's life, even as he publicly moved from one apparent success to the next, including elevation, as a British subject, to American poet laureate in 1965 and to knighthood in 1983. Bumps in the road—especially the humiliating revelation that *Encounter*, the magazine he had co-founded, had been indirectly financed by the CIA—he appeared to survive without too much visible damage.[57] In his journals, Spender criticized himself, without apparent self-pity, for living "too much . . . on the surface" and for having misplaced aspirations for literary greatness: "Instead of being a fake great man, I wanted to be a real great writer. . . . I learned from my father that it was silly to want to be Lloyd George, but how can I learn that it is silly to want to be Beethoven or Shakespeare?"[58] The problem was that he loved being a poet and especially being such a public one. Spender freely admitted that his heart jumped whenever he read his name in a newspaper. But he was equally haunted by the idea that perhaps no one really read his work.[59] And he was pursued by the thought that he might have wasted his potential, that "pleasure-seeking, frivolous, ever ready to fall in with other people's wishes," he had done too much traveling, reviewing, editing, talking, rather than spending time creating poems. He had exchanged his youthful guilt—over not meeting his parents' expectations and rebelling against their puritan inhibitions—for the guilt of not being a greater writer than he was, a guilt toward the profession. He had become a poet of surfaces, not of substance.[60]

But Spender also knew that that other type of poetry, in which the poet confronts the horror of everyday reality and retreats into a cellar to "sup off his raw and bleeding metaphors," was not for him: "I prefer the poets who are reticent, who wear the uniform of a kind of life which has some non-poetic status."[61] In *The Struggle of the Modern*, his elegant meditation on poetry and society, Spender distinguishes the "recognizers" of what he calls "the modern situation" (by which he meant, in the most general sense, attentiveness to the world outside of the world of poetry, the "idiom of the street") from the "non-recognizers"—poetic traditionalists, for whom writing and reading poetry are a superior way of living one's life: "The poetic is elevated into a grail, the pursuit of which conjures up many ladies and gentlemen modelling their lives, or a corner of their lives, on an image" suggested by poetry. Throughout *Poems Written Abroad*, Spender flirts with this idea of the unsullied poetic life, but that fantasy is constantly interrupted by the poet's own ironic sensibilities. Modernism challenged the idea of poetry as an antidote to ordinary life, but Spender also believed that, in the hands of the likes of Eliot and Pound, it had remained the language of the literary elites. Writing at the end of modernism, Spender saw an opportunity for himself, for the kind of poetry he knew he could write: "a deliberate, conscious, limited, cautious poetry of experiences." It would, in my view, not be too much of a stretch to see him rehearsing such caution in his earliest poems.[62]

Spender's mentor Auden was perhaps more successful in turning intimate reflection into a quasi-public idiom—one need to think only of poems such as "Consider" (1930) or "Here war is harmless like a monument" (1939).[63] But Spender's reluctance to overrate the capacities of the poet, while he was still holding on to the idea (a "naïve" one, by some accounts)[64] that poetry is somehow necessary to the way we live our lives, does not make Spender "irrelevant," as Stephen Metcalf has complained.[65] It doesn't really matter that Spender—concerned about his wife, whose boundary-setting interventions in his life he apparently needed—was less than candid about his continuing homosexual affairs. Andrew O'Hagan has accused Spender of being a "muddy" thinker.[66] But in his poetry, he was clear in his own way, and it is perhaps in the directness with which he attended to his inner ambivalences and weaknesses as a poet and as a human being that Spender's real and lasting achievement lies.

In one of the most perceptive comments about Spender's work, Helen Vendler called him the "poet . . . of timeless nostalgic space," an elegist entirely free of the self-righteousness of some of his peers.[67] I would add that he was an elegist for the coherent sense of self that he never had. In *The Backward Son* (1940), an underappreciated novel about his days in public school, Spender describes his early sense of detachment from other people: "Nothing of all this life was himself. He was a spectator who remained outside, and his very anxiety to become what was so foreign to him only emphasized his own separateness." Like an actor, he learned his exits and entrances, but he never became comfortable with his role, anticipating failure every day, fearing that some "new punishment was waiting on some new failure." Later in life, when he was welcomed into the Bloomsbury circle and learned to converse with the likes of T. S. Eliot and W. H. Auden, the "wall of ice" that shut him off from other people finally seemed to melt. Watching these writers, recognizing their characteristics and peculiarities, gave him a sense of being swept up by a wave of literary talent bigger than anything he could have offered himself.[68]

But although some of the exterior walls were gone, the inner barriers remained. If Virginia Woolf, cocooned in her life of literary and cultural privilege, according to Spender never knew "how it felt to be someone else," Spender never really learned how to be himself.[69] One episode he recalls in his autobiography encapsulates perhaps more movingly and more devastatingly than anything else the cause of Spender's emotional troubles. In fact, this experience became, I would argue, the enabling ground of his poetry, a lament for something or someone he never had. During an air raid in Norfolk, when he was barely seven, a soldier picked up young Stephen and carried him from his family's house in Sheringham to safety in some dug-out on the cliffs: "As he did this, he held me to his heart with a simplicity which my parents with their fears for health and morals, and their view that any uninhibited feeling was dangerous, could scarcely show."[70]

Notes

1. Spender, "Poètes Maudits," in *Dolphins* (*D* 18–29). Spender's treatment of the tempestuous relationship between Rimbaud and the much older Verlaine, who had abandoned wife and child for his much younger lover, serves as an obvious foil for his own relationships with younger men. Throughout this introduction and the notes, I will refer to Stephen Spender as "Spender" when I am addressing the poet and as "Stephen" when I am discussing the experiences of his younger self, though the boundaries between the two are, of course, fluid.

2. See p. 93 of this edition.

3. *The Augustan Books of Poetry*, binding by Stephen Spender [London: Ernest Benn, n. d.], Lilly Library; *Nine Experiments by S. H. S.: Being Poems Written at the Age of Eighteen* [Frognal, Hampstead: privately printed by S. H. S. [Stephen Harold Spender] in 30 copies, 1928]; W. H. Auden, *Poems* (Oxford: privately printed by S. H. S. [Stephen Harold Spender] in 45 copies, 1928).

4. See Yarnall's obituary in *The Washington Post*, September 12, 1989. On June 17, 1965, Yarnall reminded Randall that he had bought Spender's manuscript from him "ten or more years ago" (Lilly Library).

5. David Randall to John N. Yarnall, June 8, 1963, carbon copy, Lilly Library.

6. John N. Yarnall to David Randall, August 13, 1965, Lilly Library.

7. Spender to John N. Yarnall, March 13, 1964, August 5 and 14, 1964, Lilly Library.

8. T. S. Eliot, "Tradition and the Individual Talent" (1919), *Selected Prose of T. S. Eliot*, ed. Frank Kermode (London: Faber and Faber, 1975) 41.

9. "The Family Story-Teller: Mr. Harold Spender's New Novel," *T. P.'s Weekly*, March 6, 1914; "Readable Novels—*The Call of the Siren*," *The Spectator*, April 5, 1913.

10. Harold Spender collected Violet's poetry after her death in *The Path to Caister and Other Poems by Violet Spender, with a Word before by Harold Spender* (London: Published for Harold Spender by Sidgwick and Jackson, 1922). "Epitaph" appears on p. 67.

11. Spender, "The Ambitious Son," *NCP* 171–73.

12. *WWW* 361, 355, 12, 317. But see Spender's *roman à clef* about his childhood, *The Backward Son* (London: Hogarth, 1940): "Some were crucified not with nails, but being tied to the cross. But no. He would still feel the tearing of the ropes against his wrists. . . ." (176).

13. While the finding aid of the Bodleian lists the title of Spender's draft as *Miss Pangbourne*, Spender himself called it *Miss Pangborne*, and I have adopted his spelling here.

14. Hugh David, *Stephen Spender: A Portrait with Background* (London: Heinemann, 1922) 53.

15. The following account relies on the typescript of Spender's unfinished novel *Miss Pangborne* in the Bodleian Library, Spender Ms. 23. See *MP*, chapter VIII, January 1, 1997, 2.

16. For a description of "Susan Sled's" suicide and its effect on "Martin" (Stephen), see *MP*, chapter II, January 1, 1997, 3; chapter III, January 1, 1997, 1; chapter VIII, January 1, 1997, 4.

17. *MP*, chapter VIII, January 1, 1997, 5, 6.

18. *MP*, chapter III, January 1, 1997, 7, 4.

19. *MP*, chapter VI, January 1, 1997, 6; chapter XII, January 1, 1997, 9.

20. *MP*, chapter XIII, January 1, 1997, 2.

21. Spender, "Variations on My Life: The First," *NCP* 131.

22. Spender, "Procrastination," *The Beanstalk: The University College Literary Society* 1.1 (December 1925). Quoted in John Sutherland, *Stephen Spender: The Authorized Biography* (2004; London: Penguin, 2005) 56.

23. Spender, "Sonnet," *The Beanstalk* 1.2 (March 1926): 36.

24. Spender confirmed the biographical circumstances of his letters to Sylvia Crum in a conversation with a bookseller in Atlanta, who had acquired the Crum letter from a dealer in Bristol. According to a typed, unsigned note written by the dealer and found with the letters, Miss Crum, "HIS FATHER'S MISTRESS," was so "DISTRAUGHT OVER HER RELATIONSHIP WITH HIS FATHER AND ITS FUTILITY" that she "COMMITTED SUICIDE" (Lilly Library). See also the email correspondence between Sammy Jay of Harrington Ltd., who sold the Crum letters to the Lilly Library, and Matthew Spender, May 17, 2016, generously shared with me by Matthew Spender.

25. *MP*, chapter II, January 1, 1997, 3–4; chapter XI, January 1, 1997, 1–2.

26. Spender to Sylvia [Crum], undated [1926], Lilly Library.

27. Spender to Sylvia [Crum], undated [1926], Lilly Library.

28. Spender, "The Ambitious Son," *NCP* 172.

29. *WWW* 33–34; Sutherland, *Spender* 69–70.

30. David Leeming, *Stephen Spender: A Life in Modernism* (New York; Henry Holt, 1999) 23.

31. Spender, "By the Lake," *BC* 254–55.

32. Spender, "By the Lake," *BC* 246–47.

33. Vendler, *The Art of Shakespeare's Sonnets* (Cambridge, MA: Belknap, 1997) 329; *BC* 248. Note the transposition in Richard's rendering of sonnet 71: "the sullen, surly bell" should be "the surly sullen bell."

34. *WWW* 78.

35. John N. Yarnall to David Randall, March 4, 1965, Lilly Library. See also Randall's *Report of the Rare Book Librarian, The Lilly Library, Indiana University, July 1, 1965–June 30, 1967* (Bloomington: For Bookmen of Indiana and Friends of the University, 1967) 47,

where Randall claims with even more specificity that the mysterious traveling companion later became "a member of the British parliament."

36. Arthur Rimbaud's extended prose poem *Une saison en enfer* (A Season in Hell) appeared in Brussels in 1873. Spender later characterized Rimbaud as a poet for whom poetry was not a game but an exercise in absolute sincerity, consumed by the need "to become his own poetry"—an impossible goal for Spender himself (*The Creative Element: A Study of Vision, Despair and Orthodoxy among Some Modern Writers* [London: Hamish Hamilton, 1953] 50).

37. "Six Variations," *D* 43.

38. Spender, *Love-Hate Relations: A Study of Anglo-American Literary Sensibilities* (London: Hamish Hamilton, 1974) 104.

39. Joyce Kilmer, "Trees," *Poetry* 2.5 (August 1913): 160.

40. Serving as a coda to the volume, "Epitaph on a Poet" (pp. 90–91 in this edition) superseded earlier candidates, notably "Tail-Piece" (pp. 78–79).

41. Spender, "Never being, but always at the edge of Being," *Poems* (1933), *NCP* 7–8.

42. See, for example, Rilke's "Buch vom mönchischen Leben" (Book of Monkish Life), in *Das Stunden-Buch* (1899).

43. Spender, "By the Lake," *BC* 238–39.

44. The flute-playing shepherd is a creative allusion to a passage in Beethoven's famous letter to his brothers Johann and Karl van Beethoven, October 6, 1802, generally known as the "Heiligenstadt Testament," *Briefe Beethovens*, ed. Hugo Leichtentritt (Berlin: Deutsche Bibliothek [1912]) 37.

45. Spender, "Late Stravinsky Listening to Late Beethoven" (1972/1985), *NCP* 323–24.

46. Spender, "I think continually of those who were truly great," *Poems* (1933), *NCP* 16–17. The title was added in *CP* 30.

47. Spender, "In 1929," *NCP* 10–11.

48. Spender, "Who live under the shadow of a war," *Poems* (1933), *NCP* 12; "After they have tired of the brilliance of cities," *Poems* (1933), *NCP* 17; "Missing My Daughter" (1954), *NCP* 270.

49. Spender, "Your body is stars whose million glitter here," *Poems* (1933), *NCP* 13–14.

50. Spender, "I hear the cries of evening," *Poems* (1933); *NCP* 5. The title "Cries of Evening" was added in *CP* 197.

51. "My parents kept me from children who were rough," *Poems* (1933), *NCP* 8.

52. Spender, "Never being, but always at the edge of Being," *Poems* (1933), *NCP* 7–8; "To T.A.R.H.," *Poems* (1934), *CP* 25.

53. Spender, "Port Bou," *CP* 93–94. For the earlier, somewhat different version, published in *The Still Centre* (1939), see *NCP* 122–23.

54. Spender, "Empty House," *NCP* 252–53.

55. Spender, "Sleepless," *The Generous Days* (1971), *NCP* 299.

56. Spender, "Elegy for Margaret, VI: To J.H.S.," *CP* 152.

57. See Sutherland, *Stephen Spender* 438–46; Matthew Spender, *A House in St John's Wood: In Search of My Parents* (New York: Farrar, Straus, and Giroux, 2015) 343–55.

58. Spender, Journal, January 14, 1975, *J* 289; October 26, 1939, *J* 53.

59. Spender, Journal, February 7, 1975, *NSJ* 403; April 18, 1975, *J* 302–303.

60. Spender, Journal, April 14, 1980, *J* 401.

61. Journal, January 29, 1975, *J* 292.

62. Spender, *The Struggle of the Modern* (Berkeley: University of California Press. 1963) 164–65, 266.

63. W. H. Auden, *Collected Shorter Poems, 1927–1957* (1966; London: Faber and Faber, 1969) 49–50; 133–34 (originally titled "Here War Is Simple").

64. On Spender's "naïveté," as well as "the pith of seriousness and principle" underlying it, see Christopher Hitchens, "A Nice Bloody Fool," first published in 2005 in *The Atlantic* and collected in Hitchens, *Arguably: Essays by Christopher Hitchens* (Toronto: Signal, 2011) 332–39.

65. Stephen Metcalf, "Stephen Spender, Toady: Was There Any Substance to His Politics and Art?," *Slate*, February 7, 2005, http://www.slate.com/articles/arts/books/2005/02/stephen_spender_toady.html

66. Andrew O'Hagan, "From Soup to Fish," *The London Review of Books* (December 17, 2015): 9–10.

67. Helen Vendler, *The Music of What Happens: Poems, Poets, Critics* (Cambridge: Harvard University Press, 1988) 172.

68. Spender, *Backward Son* 61; *WWW* 182–83.

69. *WWW* 171.

70. *WWW* 202. The scene also appears in "A First War Childhood" in *Dolphins* (*D* 34–35).

A NOTE ON THE TEXT

The volume presents the text of Spender's original manuscript. While the note-book is generally in excellent shape, there is evidence that a page preceding the first poem, "Sonnet on Absence," was rather roughly removed. Since this did not affect the page numbers added by Spender himself, the page was likely ripped out by Spender himself. In addition, an unknown hand added a squiggly line and a question mark next to section 10 of "The Confession of the Monk" (p. 30), the most explicit section of the poem—perhaps a sign of disapproval by another reader?

Where Spender himself canceled a word or phrase or made a correction, only his final wording is reproduced. Emendations are limited to obvious slips of the pen. Punctuation and capitalization are expressive features and have not been al-tered, even when inconsistent and irregular. There is a great deal of ambiguity in Spender's placement of apostrophes, which is reflected in the transcriptions; in a few cases, the editor had to use his judgment. Quotation marks are added where an opening or closing quotation mark has been omitted, if the end of that quota-tion can be determined. Holographic features—such as variation in the length of dashes—are not reproduced, for the sake of better readability. In accordance with the "expanded transcription" method, no attempt is made to reproduce extraneous marks in the text or "the excessive spacing" of the original (Michael E. Stevens and Steven B. Burg, *Editing Historical Documents: A Handbook of Practice*, Walnut Creek, California: Alta Mira Press, 1997, 76).

Poems Written Abroad

Dédié comme toujours.

POEMS WRITTEN ABROAD
BY
STEPHEN SPENDER.
1927

He arrives at the town, and cares for no-
thing but his absence from home. For his host
it is difficult to entertain any affection. Al-
though for the sake of fairness it must be
admitted that he is married.

He arrives at the town, and cares for nothing but his absence from home. For his host it is difficult to entertain any affection. Although for the sake of fairness it must be admitted that he is married.

Sonnet on Absence.

Seeing me meditative - sad, my host
    Benignly smirked, and his smug tongue inclined
    To loose the drab distractions of his mind;
He brought me wine, and crisply-cheerful toast,
Then of his soured delights began to boast,
      Each tedious, flippant, dull, excuse did find
      To brighten my sad eyes (to him so blind
Searching across the sea their land's dim coast).

He took me through his country - a huge waste
    Of unexpressive beauty sans thine eyes —
      But there I saw upstand one noble tree
Pensively still, fair, kind, and queenly-graced
      Painting with quiet beauty all the skies,
      —And smiled again because I thought of thee.

                  May 1, 1927

5

Sonnet on Absence.

Seeing me meditative-sad, my host
    Benignly smirked, and his smug tongue inclined
    To loose the drab distractions of his mind;
He brought me wine, and crisply-cheerful toast,
Then of his soured delights began to boast,
    Each tedious, flippant, dull, excuse did find
    To brighten my sad eyes (to him so blind
Searching across the sea their land's dim coast).

He took me through his country—a huge waste
    Of unexpressive beauty sans thine eyes—
        But there I saw upstand one noble tree
Pensively still, fair, kind, and queenly-graced
    Painting with quiet beauty all the skies,
        —and smiled again because I thought of thee.
               May 1, 1927

He finds the town itself disappointing.
But there is a cathedral, and a chateau of
old dukes by its side which have quite an
atmosphere of their own. He sits about and
draws in the chateau gardens.

He finds the town itself disappointing. But there is a cathedral, and a chateau of old dukes by its side which have quite an atmosphere of their own. He sits about and draws in the chateau gardens.

The Chateau Garden.

In this old garden, damasked sleep
is caged, a plume-soft bird, and deep
as 'neath the sea a hole of air
is sunk (a world crushed everywhere
by grape-ripe water), is it hid
from all the vapid world outside.

The market and the stiff brass band
rush on and do not understand.
About these walls the years have past
and done no change, they went so fast.
So now two hundred years ago
I sit and watch the ladies go
with satined ruffles round the lawn,
and crisp, fat, dresses that are torn
by jealous roses. Cavaliers
rush out and swage the ladies' tears.
and are rewarded by deep blushes
that put to shame the rose bushes.

And up and down the broad escaliers

7

The Chateau Garden.

In this old garden, damasked sleep
is caged, a plume-soft bird, and deep
as 'neath the sea a hole of air
is sunk (a world crushed everywhere
by grape-ripe water), is it hid
from all the rapid world outside.
The market and the stiff brass band
rush on and do not understand.
About these walls the years have past
and done no change, they went so fast.
So now two hundred years ago
I sit and watch the ladies go
with satined ruffles round the lawn,
and crisp, fat, dresses that are torn
by jealous roses. Cavaliers
rush out and suage the ladies' tears
and are rewarded by deep blushes
that put to shame the rose bushes.
And up and down the broad escaliers

the elders go their crazy ways,
weary and weary of their duty
of nought to do but mourn lost beauty;
And in that wrath they strike their grooms
and stamp about their heartless rooms.
But all the time their souls must weep
until their paints and powders creep
thicker and thicker o'er the skin
which keeps a skeleton within.
And there are artists poets & dandies
whose narrow wit their only stand is.
All these I watch, and round the walls
waiting till the curtain falls,
poets, philosophers, and cynics
who never in the play can fix.

And up I rush, and to the town
lest the curtain should ring down;
lest while I watch time too should come
and summon _me_ with martial drum,
my trousered ghost ~~should~~ join the vision
And spoil it with anachronism.

May 8, 1927

9

the elders go their crazy ways,
weary and weary of their duty
of nought to do but mourn lost beauty;
And in that wrath they strike their grooms
and stamp about their heartless rooms.
But all the time their souls must weep
until their paints and powders creep
thicker and thicker o'er the skin
which keeps a skeleton within.
And there are artists poets & dandies
whose narrow wit their only stand is.
All these I watch, and round the walls
waiting till the curtain falls,
poets, philosophers, and cynics
who never in the play can fix.
And up I rush, and to the town
lest the curtain should ring down;
lest while I watch time too should come
and summon *me* with martial drum,
my trousered ghost then join the vision
And spoil it with anachronism.

May 8, 1927

He does not like the youth of the town, and is dejected at the staleness of beauty. He also thinks of a pleasant rhyme scheme, and a method of repeating the first phrase of a poem.

    He does not like the youth of the town,
and is dejected at the staleness of beauty.
He also thinks of a pleasant rhyme scheme,
and a method of repeating the first phrase
of a poem.

Stanzas.

I

The earth is old and sickneth of her songs;
  Eternal mother, she is tired of spring
And welcometh travail and the Winter's wrongs
  Scorning the sugared lies of them who sing.
      Nor does she care
      How summer twines her hair
      A zone for all the year
In autumn gold, and winter gold, & gold for
                    the year's king.

II

The earth is old; and the sweet nightingale
  Each year full-throated, is a mockery
Playing its part in an ironic tale:
      And none can count the many times that she
        Has seen youth's breath
        Sweet as the scented heath
        Fade, and expire in death:
Each year age hears: youth sings, and hears,
                and then must cease to be.

11

Stanzas.

I

The earth is old and sickneth of her songs;
    Eternal mother, she is tired of spring
And welcometh travail and the Winter's wrongs
    Scorning the sugared lies of them who sing.
        Nor does she care
        How summer twines her hair
        A zone for all the year
In autumn gold, and winter gold, & gold for
                  the year's king.

II

The earth is old; and the sweet nightingale
    Each year full-throated, is a mockery
Playing its part in an ironic tale:
    And none can count the many times that she
        Has seen youth's breath
        Sweet as the scented heath
        Fade, and expire in death:
Each year age hears: youth sings, and hears,
        and then must cease to be.

III

The earth is old ; sweet mortals who have sung
    In disillusion scorn me singing ; I
In vain might strike a lyre divinelier strung
    Than Virgil's ; what avails it if I die?
        Moved by deceits
        Its fickle time now greets
        The old exploréd sweets :—
The sky, the trees ; and blossom, like a poem from
                each branch rung .

IV

Bring me a bitter lyre to praise the cold ;
    And the hard crust of earth with iron frost
Bound o'er ; and veteran years that spit and scold ;
    And life and element in tempests tost ;
        And slow and slow
        The heavy years that go
        And only evil show ;
Bring me a lyre to shout belated truth, the
                earth is old .

May 15 1927.

13

III

The earth is old; sweet mortals who have sung
    In disillusion scorn me singing; I
In vain might strike a lyre divinelier strung
    Than Virgil's; what avails it, if I die?
        Moved by deceits
        Its fickle tune now greets
        The old exploréd sweets:—
The sky, the trees; and blossom, like a poem from
              each branch rung.

IV

Bring me a bitter lyre to praise the cold;
    And the hard crust of earth with iron frost
Bound o'er; and veteran years that spit and scold;
    And life and element in tempests tost;
        And slow and slow
        The heavy years that go
        And only evil show;
Bring me a lyre to shout belated truth, the
              earth is old.

May 15 1927.

There are roses in his hosts' garden,
which make him cast his mind back again,
and a delicate conceit occurs to him. But
the cast of his thought is objective and
appreciatively critical rather than personal.

There are roses in his hosts' garden,
which make him cast his mind back again,
and a delicate conceit occurs to him. But
the cast of his thought is objective and
appreciatively critical rather than personal.

She holds a rose in her two hands, and
to her face.

———————

"Why shouldst thou mock my fingers, churlish one
so fair, and so fair?
Though smooth as wax they still could pluck thy
each carmine petal, stained with the late sun   hair
they still could take.

And so the other cheek
thou offredst for my sake
being so meek?
My fingers they are paper wands
and grave, and wise;
and thou art yielding to the hands,
but what besides?
If aught, I'll have thee all. Thy face to mine:
and what hast thou to give?....but now like wine
my soul receives the fragrance thou hast given...
O ~~Art~~ 'tis no Artists' beauty, it is heaven!"

May 18, 1927

15

She holds a rose in her two hands, and
    to her face.

———————————

"Why shouldst thou mock my fingers, churlish one
so fair, and so fair?
Though smooth as wax they still could pluck thy hair
each carmine petal, stained with the late sun
they still could take.
And so the other cheek
thou offredst for my sake
being so meek?
My fingers they are paper wands
and grave, and wise;
and thou art yielding to the hands,
but what besides?
If aught, I'll have thee all. Thy face to mine:
and what hast thou to give? . . . But now like wine
my soul receives the fragrance thou hast given. . .
O 'tis no Artist's beauty, it is heaven!"
                    May 18, 1927

He is astounded by the oppressiveness of the weather, and observes it closely. After its cause has been explained by the violence of its effect, he thinks he can describe his original emotion.

He is astounded by the opprevissiveness of the weather, and observes it closely. After its cause has been explained by the violence of its effect, he thinks he can describe his original emotion.

Fragment for a possible romance. A description Before the Storm.

The sky has bent down like a cloth that sags
stretched out on four tent poles; and a great stone
that bulges in the middle, the near sun,
has robbed the intense blue of its pure tinge.
Now it is lurid yellow, and the land
an apopleptic calmness, quivering-still.
And there is silence, most morose and dumb
until its thousand furies break the earth.
The trees are sentinels in emerald green;
and blinding white the dust; and almost parched
to shiny brightness is the velvet grass.

     *   *   *

Only the swallows dart in puzzled* cubes
with sharp black wings; and an aclite-edged cry
cuts in vague figures all the poles of sound.

     *   *   *

And all so still except my ~~seething~~ heart!

     *   *   *

But see now!

        Solemnly the branches stir
in huge grey masses, moved by a slow wind.....
A slow and heavy wind that bodeth ill.

---

* ? "startled" instead of "puzzled"   May 19, 1927.
perhaps. But is it worth sacrificing
the pun on zigzag?

17

Fragment for a possible romance. A de-
scription **Before the Storm.**

The sky has bent down like a cloth that sags
stretched out on four tent poles; and a great stone
that bulges in the middle, the near sun,
has robbed the intense blue of its pure tinge.
Now it is lurid yellow, and the land
an apopleptic calmness, quivering-still.
And there is silence, most morose and dumb
until its thousand furies break the earth.
The trees are sentinels in emerald green;
and blinding white the dust; and almost parched
to shiny brightness is the velvet grass.
       *   *   *
Only the swallows dart in puzzled* cubes
with sharp black wings; and an acute-edged cry
cuts in vague figures all the poles of sound.
       *   *   *
<u>And all so still except my seething heart!</u>
       *   *   *
But see now!
      Solemnly the branches stir
In huge grey masses, moved by a slow wind. . . . .
A slow and heavy wind that bodeth ill.

---

*?"startled" instead of "puzzled"
perhaps. But it is worth sacrificing
The pun on jag saw?

May 19, 1927

Two sonnets of indignation on being accused of
reading immodest literature with the same intent
as the type of youth he dislikes cuts vulgar
paragraphs out of newspapers.

Two sonnets of indignation on being accused of
reading immodest literature with the same intent
as the type of youth he dislikes cuts vulgar
paragraphs out of newspapers.

Two Sonnets

I

I HATE, detest, and ever have despised
False beauty turned to shame by cringing lust;
Nor shall my name be wrongly criticised
And called
And ~~charged with~~ doing what it least could trust —
Because I have not ceased to mock desire,
And that I find all naked form divine,
And shameless honesty a cleansing fire,
Your thoughts have found their evil taint in mine.

Youth sickens me when 'tis a growth I know
Corporeal, gross, and keen lust to pursue;
Yet levelling nature makes one half not so
But loving, high-aspiring, and most true;
  Then let this witness what in vain I swear
  The loving is my joy, the lust my fear.

       May 21st 1927.

———————————

Two Sonnets

I

I HATE, detest, and ever have despised
False beauty turned to shame by cringing lust;
Nor shall my name be wrongly criticised
And I called doing what I least could trust—
Because I have not ceased to mock desire,
And that I find all naked form divine,
And shameless honesty a cleansing fire,
Your thoughts have found their evil taint in mine.

Youth sickens me when 'tis a growth I know
Corporeal, gross, and keen lust to pursue;
Yet levelling nature makes one half not so
But loving, high-aspiring, and most true;
       Then let this witness what in vain I swear
       The loving is my joy, the lust my fear.
               May 21st 1927.

II

I SHALL PROTEST against this martyrdom,
For Heaven is Hell if you would make it so,
And my fair state to lower state may come
If in men's eyes my beauty fall so low;
All men are creatures of vicinity,
And to their neighbours' thoughts, react or mould —
To fiery thoughts my mind is turned by thee
Even now, which in my breast had long lain cold,

                    burn
But if it cease to ~~strike~~ my heart shall say : —
"Condemned to Hell, sin is thine only pleasure,
And that sweet thing is lawfully thrown thy way
Now thou art bound within this evil measure "
        And so I'd fall, because to sin is better
        Than be called sinning, doing no such matter.*

                                    May 22nd 1927

II

I SHALL PROTEST against this martyrdom,
For Heaven is Hell if you would make it so,
And my fair state to lower state may come
If in men's eyes my beauty fall so low;
All men are creatures of vicinity,
And to their neighbours' thoughts, react or mould—
To fiery thoughts my mind is turned by thee
Even now, which in my breast had long lain cold,

But if it cease to burn my heart shall say:—
"Condemned to Hell, sin is thine only pleasure,
And that sweet thing is lawfully thrown thy way
Now thou art bound within this evil measure"
    And so I'd fall, because to sin is better
    Than be called sinning, doing no such matter.*
            May 22nd 1927

*This line revised reads "Than be called sinning, doing no such matter."

II

This poem was written, the first thirteen
verses May 26th, the next four May 27th,
the last three May 28th 1927.

This poem was written, the first thirteen
verses May 26th, the next four May 27th,
the last three May 28th 1927.

The Confession of the Monk struck blind by lightening.

1

What shall I say, and how make this confession?
    Truth only guide me, that be all my art;
Of dancing phrases I need no procession
    But that the pourings of my brooding heart
    Straightly and fully to all men impart.
Then will their souls do what mine doeth now
    (But happier than mine, since their's clearly
And to their Saviour's gracious councils' bow   [start)
For through their minds, not pains, this mercy they shall know.

2

For lo! this mercy is a riven sword;
    To silence lies, he plucks the babbling tongue;
And blindeth men that they may see His Word;
    Thus to me too, He did a gracious wrong
    Who thank him for my darkness with this song.
Yet hath he gentler ways for less vile deeds
    And he who strives to Him shall need no thorn.
So being warned by seeing festered weeds
He will be saved who hears this tale and heeds.

23

The Confession of the Monk struck blind by lightening.

1

What shall I say, and how make this confession?
  Truth only guide me, that be all my art;
Of dancing phrases I need no procession
    But that the pourings of my brooding heart
    Straightly and fully to all men impart.
Then will their souls do what mine doeth now
    (But happier than mine, since theirs' cleanly start)
And to their Saviour's gracious council's bow
For through their minds, not pains, His mercy they shall
  know.

2

For lo! His mercy is a riven sword;
  To silence lies, he plucks the babbling tongue;
and blindeth men that they may see His Word;
    Thus to me too, He did a gracious wrong
    Who thank him for my darkness with this song.
Yet hath he gentler ways for less vile deeds
    And he who strives to Him shall need no thnong.
So being warned by seeing festered weeds
He will be saved who hears this tale and heeds.

3

It was a Southern town whose wicked youth
    In drunken living wast the night and day :
(God give me strength to show the naked truth !)
      Of them I was the least, yet I know they
        Without my chiding and my subtle sway
Had ne'er dared that last crime and blasphemy
      To which I showed one hour the evil way.
    The day was brilliant and the sun sultry
So any walk or toil roused the blood rapidly,

4

P   But noone toiled because it was the feast
       When rose our Lord to show all men were saved,
  In mind of which now burgher, drudge & priest,
      Was free to do whatever thing he craved.
      Oh who at that sweet hour was so depraved
To spend his time else than in innocence?
      'Twas I, whose mind the evil scheme had paved
To sate our lust from other's confidence
The certain meal o'erlooked the prospect of expense.

3

It was a Southern town whose wicked youth
    In drunken living wost the night and day:
  (God give me strength to show the naked truth!)
    Of them I was the least, yet I know they
    Without my chiding and my subtle sway
Had ne'er dared that last crime and blasphemy
    To which I showed one hour the evil way.
  The day was brilliant and the sun sultry
So any walk or toil roused the blood rapidly,

4

But noone toiled because it was the feast
    When rose our Lord to show all men were saved,
In mind of which now burgher, drudge & priest,
    Was free to do whatever thing he craved.
    Oh who at that sweet hour was so depraved
To spend his time else than in innocence?
    'Twas I, whose mind the evil schemes had paved
To sate our lust from other's confidence
The certain meal o'erlooked the prospect of expense.

5

For now, would troop to where the river bends

In customary bands young men and maids,
And in short meadows which each lush tree ends

Play, tearing down the branches tinselled braids

There, all is mature peace and restful glades
Of pastoral ease; yet where the maidens vied

I planned the most imprudent of our raids

Insulting simple faith which did confide
In the fair day, the streams and peaceful countryside.

6

The river was like glass, whose vivid banks

Almost to melt into the flood did seem
So overgrown the shore with emerald ranks

Of golden-headed iris, and where gleam

The waxen lilies floating on the stream,
Till green gives place to blue where the deep waters

Reflect the sky in an intenser dream:

But little good that perfect beauty taught us
Except the more to hurt the city's trustful daughters.

27

5

For now, would troop to where the river bends
    In customary bands young men and maids,
And in short meadows which each lush tree ends
    Play, tearing down the branches tinselled braids.
    There, all is mature peace and restful glades
Of pastoral ease; yet where the maidens vied
    I planned the most imprudent of our raids
Insulting simple faith which did confide
In the fair day, the streams and peaceful countryside.

6

The river was like glass, whose vivid banks
    Almost to melt into the flood did seem
So overgrown the shore with emerald ranks
    Of golden-headed iris, and where gleam
    The waxen lilies floating on the stream,
Till green gives place to blue where the deep waters
    Reflect the sky in an intenser dream:
But little good that perfect beauty taught us
Except the more to lust the city's trustful daughters.

7

We watched the young girls resting and at play
From near the tesseled foliage of some trees,
And in what sweet content they wiled the day
Some half-reclined, some dallying with their ease;
Till suddenly my signal made it cease
As forth we leapt with cries: in vain they ran;
Each one of us his lawless prize did seize.
The dames who heard their shouts as we began
Said "Hark they play! Alas, our youth too had its span."

8

Some ran away, but soon ceased, losing breath;
Some fell, and straight were seized to be the prey;
One, with the blessed smile the saints melt death
Received her beauty's ~~gift~~ thief a nought did say,
But her calm eyes to god, not him, did pray,
At which his heart did melt & stopped his sin;
Yet he did leave us our persistent way
And to his own confession entered in,
While his loon comrades now their greatest crime begin.

29

7

We watched the young girls resting and at play
From near the tasseled foliage of some trees,
And in what sweet content they wiled the day
Some half-reclined, some dallying with their ease;
Till suddenly my signal made it cease
as forth we leapt with cries: in vain they ran;
Each one of us his lawless prize did seize.
The dames who heard their shouts as we began
Said "Hark they play! Alas, our youth too had its span."

8

Some ran away, but soon ceased, losing breath;
Some fell, and straight were seized to be the prey;
One, with the blessèd smile the saints melt death
Received her beauty's thief & nought did say,
But her calm eyes to God, not him, did pray,
At which his heart did melt & stopped his sin;
Yet he did leave us our persistent way
And to his own confession entered in,
While his boon comrades now their greatest crime begin.

But now my eyes were turned from others, where

       By my own side I thrust the indignant form

Of a dark beauty, lovelier in her fear

       With burning eyes, and deep skin turned more warm.

       With stiff little arms she kept from her my swarm

But holding her thin waist spurred my desire

       To crush against my breast that fervent storm,

And to my heart embrace the scarlet flower

Deep as a flame, to set my smouldering heart afire.

10

I pulled her face to mine and touched her lips

       Whose parched wrath met my hunger with keen scorn;

Again I pressed, and my keen hand now strips

       Her breast, round which the does her gloss a torn.

       Then as the fruit we smell to our taste sworn,

And touch the velvet skin, I kissed her face

       And then the neck, & then the breast forlorn

And cold, and lying there in snowy grace,

And with my hungry mouth passed each voluptuous place.

9

But now my eyes were turned from others, where
    By my own side I thrust the indignant form
Of a dark beauty, lovelier in her fear
    With burning eyes, and deep skin turned more
        warm.
    With stiff lithe arms she kept from her my swarm
But holding her thin waist spurred my desire
    To crush against my breast that fervent storm,
And to my heart embrace the scarlet flower
Deep as a flame, to set my smouldering heart afire.

10

I pulled her face to mine and touched her lips
    Whose parched wrath met my hunger with keen
        scorn;
Again I pressed, and my keen hand now strips
    Her breast, round which the dress hangs loose &
        torn.
    Then as the fruit we smell to our taste sworn,
And touch the velvet skin, I kissed her face
    And then the neck, & then the breast forlorn
And cold, and lying there in snowy grace,
And with my hungry mouth passed each voluptuous
    place.

11

' Yet this was seen for from the river bed
    Glanced forth Molenia the long-hidden bride
Of the lush stream, and straightway is she fled
    To grave Demeter scattering thick and wide
    The golden seeds of the next harvest-tide.
She said : "new Gods have men whom they despise"
    And showed how we our Saviour word defied
And how upon the day when he did rise
Our sin straightway again his flesh recrucifies.

12

    Then wrathful nature the clear sky clouds o'er
    And all is ghostly-still, and e'en the trees
Stand motionless as sentinels in awe
    Of Death, preparing to disturb their peace.
    The land is quivering-still, as if in lease
Of some foul apoplexy which will burst
    Its drum-stiff crust in terrible disease;
    All Heaven its deep cast blue has now dispersed
Earth, water, air, and life, are still as if accursed ..

33

11

Yet this was seen for from the river bed
 Glanced forth Molania the long-hidden bride
Of the lush stream, and straightway is she fled
  To grave Demeter scattering thick and wide
  The golden seeds of the next harvest-tide.
She said: "New Gods have men whom they despise"
  And showed how we our Saviours word defied
And how upon the day when he did rise
Our sin straightway again his flesh recrucifies.

12

then wrathful nature the clear sky clouds o'er
  And all is ghostly-still, and e'en the trees
Stand motionless as sentinels in awe
  Of Death, preparing to disturb their peace.
  The land is quivering-still, as if in lease
Of some foul apoplexy which will burst
  Its drum-stiff crust in terrible disease;
All Heaven its deep-cast blue has now dispersed
Earth, water, air, and life, are still as if accursed. . .

13

The sky has bent right down, a heavy sheet

That sags, weighed by that swift-revolving stone

The too-near sun, that turns to bilious-sweet

The lurid air; nothing does move or groan;

Only the swallows startled shapes are thrown

In rules across the sky, and many-wheres

A vague acute-edged cry, unheard, is gone

Cutting in pallid figures all our fears.

But hark! now in the trees an ominous wind stirs.

14

Then in huge masses all the foliage swayed

And ever more the hour resembled night;

And next the drooped clouds fell, and swift hail flayed

The earth in hissing shafts of splintered light.

The river was like torment to the sight

With heaving jets that sprang to meet the rain;

The plumaged trees were tossing in their fright;

Turned to a million mountains that smooth plain

the stream; and all the land seemed chaos once again.

35

13

The sky has bent right down, a heavy sheet
　　That sags, weighed by that swift-revolving stone
The too-near sun, that turns to bilious-sweet
　　The lurid air; nothing does move or groan;
　　Only the swallows startled shapes are thrown
In cubes across the sky, and many-wheres
　　A vague acute-edged cry, unheard, is gone
Cutting in pallid figures all our fears.
But hark! now in the trees an ominous wind stirs.

14

Then in huge masses all the foliage swayed
　　And ever more the hour resembled night;
And next the draped clouds fell, and swift hail flayed
　　The earth in hissing shafts of splintered light.
　　The river was like torment to the sight
With heaving jets that sprang to meet the rain;
　　The plumaged trees were tossing in their fright;
Turned to a million mountains that smooth plain
The stream; and all the land seemed chaos once again.

Meanwhile my treacherous hand in time was stayed
      Before my sin had left its first vile state ;
My lecherous limbs grew suddenly afraid
      And I was chilled by that cool blast of hate
         The wind, prelude of storm. And then too late
I saw the angry fire across the clouds
         In dazzling sheets burst forth from Heaven's gate ;
      And swift, I ran and joined the group where crowds it,
My comrades, 'gainst dark nature even darker shrouds .

      There stood we trembling for the dire revenge ;
            And not far off our victims too did creep ;   ;
      Against black nature white, hers to avenge
            Were they, but we as black 'gainst black most deep.
            And seeing us, though wronged pity must weep. nd.
      But even now we quarrelled and our hand
            To all repentant thinking still asleep
      Turned round on me who in the midst did stand
   And said "Yours was the thought, & yours the guilty
                                          Hand."

15

Meanwhile my treacherous hand in time was stayed
    Before my sin had left its first vile state;
My lecherous limbs grew suddenly afraid
    And I was chilled by that cool blast of hate
    The wind, prelude of storm. And then too late
I saw the angry fire across the clouds
    In dazzling sheets burst forth from Heaven's gate;
And swift, I ran and joined the group where crowds
My comrades, 'gainst dark nature even darker shrouds.

16

There stood we trembling for the dire revenge;
    And not far off our victims too did creep;
Against black nature white, her's to avenge
    Were they, but we as black 'gainst black most deep.
    And seeing us, though wronged pity must weep.
But even now we quarrelled and our band
    To all repentant thinking still asleep
Turned round on me who in the midst did stand
And said "Yours' was the thought, & your's the guilty hand."

17

Twas true and I did tremble. Then the sky
   With one more tearing thunder-peal was spent.
The lightning followed swift, and straight did fly
   Iona's bolt towards its hated target sent.
    I saw no more, but all my clothes were rent
And gleaming-white my naked body shone
   An alabaster pillar, the tale went.
And then a moment and the storm was gone
The other's own, and stunned, I stayed there left alone.

18

  Alone I stood, unseeing and uncared;
     Not knowing and not recking if I lived;
  My blinded eyes towards the heavens stared
     Blank as a statue's, where the clouds did lift.
      There was no thought within my mind nor drift
Of purpose: Nor how long I took my stand
     Thus stonelike I know not, until the gift
Of Heaven saved me, and I felt a hand
Steal in my arm, and throw around a surcoat's band.

17

Twas true and I did tremble. Then the sky
    With one more tearing thunder-peal was spent.
The lightning followed swift, and straight did fly
    Jove's bolt towards its hated target sent.
    I saw no more, but all my clothes were rent
And gleaming-white my naked body shone
    An alabaster pillar, the tale went.
And then a moment and the storm was gone
The other's ran, and stunned, I stayed there left alone.

18

Alone I stood, unseeing and uncared;
    Not knowing and not recking if I lived;
My blinded eyes towards the heavens stared
    Bleak as a statue's, where the clouds did lift.
    There was no thought within my mind nor drift
Of purpose: Nor how long I took my stand
    Thus stonelike I know not, until the gift
Of Heaven saved me, and I felt a hand
Steal in my arm, and throw around a surcoat's band.

It led me down to where beside the bank
  A boat lay heaving in the sullen stream
Still restless from the storm; it had half-sunk
  Beneath the rain, and thus delayed I ween
  Was there to save me; then, as in a dream
Her soft voice spoke, and O it was I swear
  The voice of her I'd wronged which sweet
                                         / did seem
As kind-lipped roses; she alone did care
To lead me to her Heaven, and from the Hell left there.

She took me to the Abbey whose kind saints
  Received me in. Against the boat's rough
                                         / keel
The water crunches as its way it paints;
  The air was light now, & my flesh could feel
  The wind caress my face and gently heal
With its cool balsam. From its radiant skies
  The sun, now westering, 'gainst my head did
                                         / steal
Like lurking wings, & as the frail boat lies
                                    sightless
Besides, the quay, its warmth caressed my eyes. /

FINIS

19

It led me down to where beside the bank
    A boat lay heaving in the sullen stream
Still restless from the storm; it had half-sunk
    Beneath the rain, and thus delayed I wean
    Was there to save me; then, as in a dream
Her soft voice spoke, and O it was I swear
    The voice of her I'd wronged which sweet did seem
As kind-lipped roses; she alone did care
To lead me to her Heaven, and from the Hell left there.

20

She took me to the Abbey whose kind saints
    Received me in. Against the boat's rough keel
The water crunches as its way it paints;
    The air was light now, & my flesh could feel
    The wind caress my face and gently heal
With its cool balsam. From its radiant skies
    The sun, now westering, 'gainst my head did steal
Like brushing wings, & as the frail boat lies
Besides the quay, its warmth caressed my sightless eyes.

FINIS

Song

Flowers will I ~~give~~ *bring* for thy hair, my love
    To ~~color~~ *vary* its gold ;
A coral to ~~think~~ from each, ear, my love,
    And ~~bracelets~~ *hang* to hold
Thy frail wrists in a saffron zone .
    Each delight thou choosest to wear, my love
        Thou shalt have ; & when old and alone
In *this* thou shalt still be fair, my love,
        Though the poet *be* gone .

                  June 1 '27 .

43

Song

Flowers will I bring for thy hair, my love
    To vary its gold;
A coral to hang from each ear, my love,
    And bracelets to hold
The frail wrists in a saffron zone.
Each delight thou choosest to wear, my love
    Thou shalt have; & when old and alone
In *this* thou shalt still be fair, my love
    Though the poet be gone.

June 1 '27.

To a Poet.

Beloved musician, I will ~~give~~ my lyre
    For the strong playing of thy fingers' skill,
To strike the deeper chords, and then the wire
    More deft than I, till chaos linger shrill
Into the thinner ecstasies of light;
    Far more obedient be it to thy mind
      (unnurtured)   ~~valuing~~ for it needs
Than mine ∧ ~~being sold~~, ~~and worthy of such~~ might,
    Possessing notes of ocean, and of wind;
So take it till with sure, maturer touch,
    (Learnt from thy playing) of my tender hand,
I give back thanks with a sweet note & such
    As answereth thee; for thou wilt understand.
Play on it now, this instrument my heart
Which I lend thee, till I take up my part.

June 12 '27

45

To a Poet.

Beloved musician, I will give my lyre
  For the strong playing of thy fingers' skill,
To strike the deeper chords, and then the wire
  More deft than I, till chaos linger shrill
Into the thinner ecstasies of light;
  Far more obedient be it to thy mind
Than mine (unnurtured), for it needs such might,
  Posessing notes of ocean, and of wind,
So take it till with sure, maturer touch,
  (Learnt from the playing) of my tender hand,
I give back thanks with a sweet note & such
  As answereth thee; for thou wilt understand.
Play on it now, this instrument my heart
Which I lend thee, till I take up my part.

June 12 '27

Bluebeard   The boy who was called "the Night-
ingale" for his lovely singing & his beauty.
A

1

O lovely boy, with the undaunted head
What shall I call thee? Hyacinth for thy eyes
Or lily for thy pose, crowned by the fair
And falling glory of thy auburn hair?

2

Nature said,
Who from her streams did rise
And bless thy mother's bed: —
" We will throw violets, roses, speedwell
Upon thy babe, and such sweet minstrelsies
So will make all these perish, and excel
His voice the perfumed-singing nightingale."

3

The perfum faery voice
Had such melodious noise
That at its sweet suspended note
The neighbours all would say: " That throat
" So white, and bellied like the plumes
" Of some chaste swan of no man comes;

4

" It is a nightingale's, when the wan moon
" Has passed her fingers over the dazed feathers
" Puckering & fawning in their unearthly swoon."

47

The boy who was called "the Night-
ingale" for his lovely singing & his beauty.

A

1

O lovely boy, with the undaunted head
What shall I call thee? Hyacinth for thy eyes
Or lily for thy pose, crowned by the fair
And falling glory of thy auburn hair?

2

Nature said,
Who from her streams did rise
And bless thy mother's bed:—
"We will throw violets, roses, speedwell
Upon thy babe, and such sweet minstrelsies
As will make all these perish, and excel
His voice the perfumed-singing nightingale."

3

The faery voice
Had such melodious noise
That at its sweet suspended note
The neighbours all would say: "That throat
"So white, and bellied like the plumes
"Of some chaste swan of no man comes;

4

"It is a nightingale's, when the wan moon
"Has passed her fingers over the dazed feathers
"Puckering & fanning in their unearthly swoon."

And then, in a minute's gossip talk,
Like those bewildered weathers
Tumbling on Ulysses and his old crew
Out fell the secret of how Nature threw
Her vivid treasures
Upon this lovely boy. The neighbours' tale
Did seal his name - it was "the Nightingale!"

June 13.

5

And then, in a minute's gossip talk,
Like those bewildered weathers
Tumbling on Ulysses and his old crew
Out fell the secret of how Nature threw
Her vivid treasures
Upon this lovely boy. The neighbours' tale
Did seal his name—it was "the Nightingale!"

June 13.

The Boy the Nightingale, as good
as he was gold, one morning stood
Inside the churchyard where the graves
Are round and neat, as when the waves
In summer, smooth the sea's deep hair
For hid beneath the water there.
In bright cascades of many a gem
Towards his mouth the birds all came
Thinking his coral lips were berries
as red and ripe as any cherries.
The oily trees towards him flowed
Thinking his hair the sun that glowed,
and being darkened by that shade
the little flowers all shook, afraid,
and then, towards him in a twinkle
leapt swiftly with bright heads that tinkle.
For always where he went, the sound
Of music to his heart was found

And all things the accompaniment
Became of that sweet instrument.
And to those bright violins this song
From his blythe heart today was sung :—

SONG

"Flowers will rain for thy hair, my love,
To crown its gold:
A coral to hang from each ear, my love,
And bracelets to hold
the frail wrists in a soft iron ore.
Each delight thou choosest to wear, my love,
thou shalt have, when old & alone
In this thou shalt still be fair, my love
Though the poet be gone."

June 16 - 17 - 18

51

B

The Boy the Nightingale, as good
As he was gold, one morning stood
Inside the churchyard where the graves
Are round and neat, as when the waves
In summer, smooth the sea's deep hair
Far hid beneath the water there.
In bright cascades of many a gem
Towards his mouth the birds all came
Thinking his coral lips were berries
as red and ripe as any cherry's.
The oily trees towards him flowed
Thinking his hair the sun that glowed,
and being darkened by that shade
The little flowers all shook, afraid,
And then, towards him in a twinkle
Leapt swiftly with bright heads that tinkle.
For always where he went, the sound
Of music to his heart was bound

And all things were accompaniment
To his sweet voice the instrument,
And swift violins like silver rain
Played subtly in his worried brain
Until the thought blushed like a rose
On his rich lips which did unclose
Divinely pouting as the flowers
Which fill with fragrant tunes their bowers.
There is no tune as faintly rung
From nodding flower-beds as he sung...
His song which was the fleur-de-lys
And sparkling snow & live diamonds freeze,
And all the grass & wind & streams
And waters where the iris gleams
The rainbows, rain & the wild air —
O let us leave him singing there!

And all things were accompaniment
To his sweet voice the instrument,
And swift violins like silver rain
Played subtly in his woried brain
Until the thought blushed like a rose
On his rich lips which did unclose
Divinely-pouting as the flowers
Which fill with fragrant tunes their bowers.
There is no tune as feintly rung
From nodding flower-beds as he sung. . .
His song which was the fleur-de lys
And sparkling snow where diamonds freeze,
And all the grass, & wind & streams
And waters where the iris gleams,
The rainbows, rain & the wild air—
O let us leave him singing there!

      June 16–17–18

The original
Bluebeard, Gilles de Rais of Brittany

Gilles de Rais'
Face,
More blue the fringes shone!
The tassels were
Torn from the air
(The sky is made of silk there).
Below that sun
The fringe was smeared,
O no one heard
His step but stared
And turned right round and said
"O Gilles de Rais'
                    Face,
                        And beard!"

June 15·16·17·18·19

The original
Bluebeard, Gilles de Rais of Brittany

Gilles de Rais'
Face,
How blue the fringes shone!
The tassels were
Torn from the air
(The sky is made of silk there).
Below that sun
The fringe was smeared.
O no one heard
His step but stared
And turned right round and said
"O Gilles de Rais'
                Face,
                        And beard!"

                June 15–16–17–18–19

Written after the fête le Dieu at Nantes (June 16) on
    June 17th.

Francis, who knit the world in one great bond
        Of brotherhood for Man, & Beasts, & Things,
            Witness my vow, who find men are not kings
But bound to Beast and Earth by ties o'erfond:
I shall remember in this Christian land
            How I have seen such acts of cruelty
            To brothers Ox, and lamb, as change to pity
Grim brother steel, held in the axeman's hand;
    And ~~finding~~ there the same,
~~I shall remember, and~~ my heart shall turn
            To Christians massacred by Pagan laws,
        martyrs
            and Christians thrown to lions back to back,
and ~~christians~~ over great fires made to burn;
        And I shall think of how at Death's cold jaws
            Christ's great heart broke so loud men heard
                                    it crack.
                                June 16.

55

Written after the fête de Dieu at Nantes (June 16) on
June 17th.

Francis, who knit the world in one great bond
   Of brotherhood for Man, & Beasts, & Things,
   Witness my vow, who find men are not kings
But bound to Beast and Earth by ties o'erfond:
I shall remember in this Christian land
   How I have seen such acts of cruelty
   To brothers Ox, and Lamb, as change to pity
Grim brother steel, held in the axeman's hand;
And finding there the same, my heart shall turn
   To Christians massacred by Pagan laws,
     And Christians thrown to lions back to back,
And martyrs over great fires made to burn;
   And I shall think of how at Death's cold jaws
     Christ's great heart broke so loud men heard
                  it crack.
              June 16.

A Sonnet to be beautifully printed at the beginning
of his poems.

The night was clear, and all the frosted sky
    Spread pale as wine around the living moon;
    Whose sad, beneficence like milk did swoon
Across the hills; their fleecy backs ~~did the~~ on high
Worpt as sheep, ~~till~~ darkening to huge shapes
    Cleft black between, where the great valleys lay;
    There was no sound to take that peace away,
No movement to disturb those slumbering rhythms:
Yet mocking the purpurean dome – a bird
   . That is a poem's birth – a Thought did mar
The sky's all-vacant quiet, and deeply ~~heard~~ stirred
    Reflecting in my mind, a voice from far, –
The Night, that whispered to the Earth ~~the unheard~~ : –
    "Do you not see my new, my ~~baby~~ star?"
                 youngest
            June 22.

A Sonnet to be beautifully printed at the beginning
of his poems.

The night was clear, and all the frosted sky
        Spread pale as wine around the living moon;
        Her sad beneficence like milk did swoon
Across the hills, whose fleecy backs on high
As white as sheep, darkening to huge abysms
        Cleft black bettween, where the great valleys lay;
        There was no sound to take that peace away,
No movement to disturb those slumbering rhythms:
Yet mocking the purpurean dome—a bird
        That is a poem's birth—a Thought did mar
The sky's all-vacant quiet, and deeply stirred
        Reflecting in my mind, a voice from far,—
The Night, that whispered to the Earth unheard:—
        "Do you not see my new, my youngest star?"
                        June 22.

After Ronsard.

AS WHEN IN MAY we see the budding rose
    In its young beauty, in its primal flower,
    Make the sky jealous in the unfolding hour
When dawn her daybreak tears upon it throws:
Its fragile petals, grace, and love enclose,
    Its scent perfumes the trees, and every bower,
    But by the rains, or heats' excessive power
Withers, it dies and each slow leaf does lose:
    So, at thy first and young awakening
    When earth and heaven thy loveliness did sing,
Fate killed thee, and the grave thy corse encloses.
    For obsequy then, take these tears of ours,
    This vase with milk, this basket filled with
So live, or dead, thy body be all roses.   / flowers,

                   June 24.

After Ronsard.

AS WHEN IN MAY we see the budding rose
    In its young beauty, in its primal flower,
    Make the sky jealous in the unfolding hour
When dawn her daybreak tears upon it throws:
Its fragile petals grace, and love enclose,
    Its scent perfumes the trees, and every bower,
    But by the rain's, or heat's excessive power
Withered, it dies and each slow leaf does lose:
    So, at thy first and young awakening
    When Earth and heaven thy loveliness did sing,
Fate killed thee, and the grave thy corse encloses.
    For obsequy then, take these tears of ours,
    This vase with milk, this basket filled with flowers,
So live, or dead, thy body be all roses.

<u>June 24.</u>

Tail-piece.

In the middle of the day
I was suddenly seized with a great weariness.
My eyes refused my book, and I flung myself on my bed,
And although unable to sleep I breathed like one sleeping.
I imagined vaguely the great lawn-bank of the tree
outside my ~~window~~ bedroom window.
And I heard the birds singing,
And there was a music or philosophie as rich perfumes,
which made me think :——
'How easily now a great hand might put me to sleep,
  and I go on lying in this delicious melancholy for
  ever;"
O where am I, my love, in my grave, or dead and
white-limbed?"
  And the cities and earthly beauties I had longed for sank
  back into the milkwhite horizon of my mind.
"Caressing hand, let me sleep now for infinity,
  And forget the anguish of beauty, and the anxieties
  of pleasure!" I said.
                                        June 30.

61

Tail-piece.

In the middle of the day
I was suddenly seized with a great weariness.
My eyes refused my book, and I flung myself on my bed,
And although unable to sleep I breathed like one sleeping.
I imagined vaguely the great lawn-bark of the tree
outside my bedroom window.
And I heard the birds singing,
And there was a music as philosophic as rich perfumes,
which made me think:—
"How easily now a great hand might put me to sleep,
and I go on lying in this delicious melancholy for
ever;
O where am I, my love, in my grave, or dead and
white-limbed?"
And the cities and earthly beauties I had longed for sank
back into the milkwhite horizon of my mind.
"Caressing hand, let me sleep now for infinity,
And forget the anguish of beauty, and the anxieties
of pleasure!" I said.

June 30.

The Ballad of Money.

1

When I return to London, these mountains still will stand
In virgin blue, and still the lake reflect the shadowed land,
Her dress as pale and quivering, by little breezes fanned.

2

But Southwards of Geneva, the bluest waters lie
With such intense a loveliness as makes the spirit cry
longing to burst away from flesh, & have a poet's eye.

3

And across the seas is beauty that I shall never know
The East as warm and vivid as flame, and where the snow
Is one white-blinding wall, seen by the esquimo.

4

Far-held from me these secrets, but most close by the years
Which lock fast Rome, and Egypt where Cleopatra's tears
Are turned to pearls, and rubies her blood, the harlot wears.

5

For there are things I shall not see, nor that yet fairer day
When men with tongues of silver, and heart & faces gay
Along the streets of Athens would go their mained way.

6

This life excelled earth's beauty; as to did England's time
When Drake across deep oceans sought a far fabled clime
And still a richer treasure, Shakespeare revealed his rhyme.

63

The Ballad of Money.

I

When I return to London, these mountains still will stand
In virgin blue, and still the lake reflect the shadowed land,
Her dress as pale and quivering, by little breezes fanned.

2

But Southwards of Geneva, the bluest waters lie
With such intense a loveliness as makes the spirit cry
Longing to burst away from flesh, & have a poet's eye.

3

And across the seas is beauty that I shall never know
The East as warm and vivid as flame, and where the snow
Is one white-blinding wall, seen by the esquimo.

4

Far-held from me these secrets, but most close by the years
Which lock fast Rome, and Egypt where Cleopatra's tears
Are turned to pearls, and rubies her blood, the harlot wears.

5

For these are things I shall not see, nor that yet fairer day
When men with tongues of silver, and hearts & faces gay
Along the streets of Athens would go their married way.

6

This life excelled earth's beauty; as too did England's time
When Drake across deep oceans sought a far-fabled clime
And still a richer treasure, Shakespeare revealed his rhyme.

Till

~~But~~ that which was the booty became our only prize;
The poetry and adventure were mocked at by the wise
Who nearer home to Money their sudden sacrifice.

For Eldorado's jewels were sparkling things to hold
And lustful is the shining of swiftly-pouring gold;
And yet the gleam of diamonds is heartless and most cold.

With mouths that suck & pucker we cling to her great breasts,
Her flanks are gold, & crushed beneath the sudden monster rests
The men whom man has conquered to serve her proud beheads.

10

And the suppliant scorns nature and spoils her floating ways
And keepeth back his neighbour to where the golden—rays;
Forgotten art thou Beauty, the love of other days.

O is ~~not she~~ too beautiful to stay and comes not near?
As when that voice called "Adam, O Adam doest thou hear
And girt about with leaves, Men crept away in fear.

July 14.

7

Till that which was the booty became our only prize;
The poetry and adventure were mocked at by the wise
Who nearer home to Money their goddess sacrifice.

8

For Eldorado's jewels were sparkling things to hold
And lustful is the shining of swiftly-pouring gold;
And yet the gleam of diamonds is heartless and most cold.

9

With mouths that suck & pucker we cling to her great
    breasts;
Her flanks are gold, & crushed beneath the goddess-
    monster rests
The men whom man has conquered to serve her proud
    behests.

10

And the suppliant scorns nature and spoils her fleeting
    ways
And keepeth back his neighbour to where the goddess—
    pays;
Forgotten art thou Beauty, the love of other days.

11

O is he not too beautiful to stay and comes not near?
    x   x   x   x   x
As when a voice called "Adam, O Adam doest thou hear"
And girt about with leaves, Man crept away in fear.

                July 14.

Clair de lune

The moon ~~has~~ spilt
her milk
In silver fountains
across the mountains —
Until like silk
It falls ~~across~~ my knee, the poet.
Nor do I ~~sing~~ alone, for Romeo
Does he ~~not~~ lean from this high ~~his~~ balcony
And speak to Juliet?
And does not Aeneas watch the Alpenglow
fade, fade, from this high poop where slow
Burns his fair love, his love, the queen Dido?
~~And~~ ~~the~~ music that clangs

I cannot tell
Whether it is ~~the~~ a madrigal
~~That~~ Strings the fretted leaves ~~of~~
That Mozart plays ~~so fast~~; or slow
The heart-apalling swell
Of Beethoven
In the valley
—Deep —
below.
~~But~~ See Stravinsky on the snow
Saw the white air ~~and~~ yet again
The Goodly John Sebastian
Who moves the golden stars about their queen.
Their queen,
Oh baby moon.

67

Clair de lune

The moon has spilt
her milk
In silver fountains
across the mountains—
Until like silk
It falls across my knee, the poet.
Nor do I stand alone, for Romeo
Does he not lean from this high balcony
And speak to Juliet?
And does not Aeneas watch the Alpenglow
Fade, fade, from this high poop where slow
Burns his fair love, his love, the queen Dido?
This music that clangs
I cannot tell
Whether it is a madrigal
Stirring the fretted leaves
That Mozart plays; or slow
The heart-apalling swell
of Beethoven
In the valley
—Deep—
Below.
See Stravinksy on the snow
Saw the white air and yet again
the Goodly John Sebastian
Who moves the golden stars about their queen.
Their queen,
Oh moon.

To   W. E. P.

That thou art ill does gloom me like a cloud
        That has obscured the mountains and the sky,
And ~~stifled~~ choked the maiden Day in a black shroud
                  swift
        And made ~~fast~~ waters stiff & frozen lie;
Now all things follow to their contraries;
        Not cold but healing warmth should fill the,
                                          day;
Not these stark boughs but foliage-loden trees
        Across deep summer skies their wealth should
                                          sway.

How shall we remedy this vile distress?
        How woo the Sun to mount again his throne?
How bend the corn with grain to gild and bless?
        What means will bring back Summer to her crown?
There is but one; that thou shouldst come & tell
The lingering fields thou livest, and art well.

                        July 27

69

To W.E.P.

That thou art ill does gloom me like a cloud
    That has obscured the mountains and the sky,
And choked the maiden Day in a black shroud
    And made swift waters stiff & frozen lie;
Now all things follow to their contraries;
    Not cold but healing warmth should fill the day,
Not these stark boughs but foliage-laden trees
    Across deep summer skies their wealth should sway.

How shall we remedy this vile distress?
    How woo the sun to mount again his throne?
How bend the corn with grain to gild and bless?
    What means will bring back Summer to her own?
There is but one; that thou shouldst come & tell
The lingering fields thou livest, and art well.

July 27

Consolation of Dust.

1

If I have followed thee across the seas,
    And kissed the mountains, thy rich-swelling breast,
And loved thy hair the clouds, thy breath, the breeze
    Thy body the dark East, thy soul the West ;

2

If in the ragged Eden of my mind,
    Thy golden light has shattered all the lust;
If in a women, in a book, a friend,
    I have pursued thee through the dark & dust

3

Most vivid, O most brilliant, most divine,
    love, virtue,
    Women, and light, and art, and all my toil,
    earth of
Oh changing beauty, wilt thou then be mine
    And lift me from thyself and from thy soil.

4

        then
.... No, I will die thy lover, cruel god!.;
                          ive ease
    But in thy dazed and self-reflected love;
Thou still must hear a Dust beneath thy sad
    Dining thy passionless eternities.

July 23

Consolation of Dust.

89

If I have followed thee across the seas,
  And kissed the mountains, thy rich-swelling breast,
And loved thy hair the clouds, thy breath, the breeze
  Thy body the dark East, thy soul the West;

2

If in the ragged Eden of my mind,
  Thy golden light has shattered all the lust;
If in a woman, in a book, a friend,
  I have pursued thee through the dark & dust

3

Most vivid, O most brilliant, most divine,
  Love, virtue, light, and art, and all my toil,
Oh earth of beauty, wilt thou then be mine
  And lift me from thyself and from thy soil?

4

. . . . Then I will die thy lover, cruel god!;
  But in thy dazed and self-reflective ease
Thou still must hear a Dust beneath thy sod
  Living thy passionless eternities.

July 23

Epitaph on a poet.

They said my life was wild; but still I led it
(A haltered lion) to the very end:
I had a word to say, and having said it
        Turned back to Death again, my
                only friend.

                        Iuf 26

Epitaph on a poet.

They said my life was wild; but still I led it
    (A haltered lion) to the very end;
I had a word to say, and having said it
    Turned back to Death again, my
          only friend.
July 26

EXPLANATORY NOTES

For full bibliographical details of works cited in the notes, consult the list of abbreviations or the bibliography.

About the Notebook

Spender used a notebook he had acquired in France to record his poems. Several pages bear the watermark of the Vidalon Paper Mills, founded in the sixteenth century near Annonay, France, by the Vidalon family. Some of the watermarks are in the shape of the manufacturer's coat of arms, a crown-topped shield that depicts a hot air balloon and a scroll, above a banner that reads "Ite per Orbem," "Travel the world." The motto is a reference to the Montgolfier family, who had taken over Vidalon in 1693; Étienne and Joseph Montgolfier used Vidalon paper for the hot air balloon they constructed and then flew publicly for the first time in 1782. Subsequently known as "Canson," after Barthélémy de Canson who had married Etienne's daughter, the company continues to produce fine paper for use by artists today.

Dédié comme tojours

"Dedicated, as always": Leaving the name of the recipient blank, while also suggesting, in a language not his own, that this might not be his first poetic effort, perfectly encapsulates the volatile state of Stephen's mind at the time: confused and confident, jejune yet eager to make an impression.

He arrives . . .

"He arrives at the town . . .": The "town" is Nantes, described by Spender as "a grey stone provincial town, with a third of its population always dressed in mourning for some far-removed deceased cousin" (*WWW* 33).

"For his host it is difficult to entertain any affection": The host is the Protestant "pasteur" in whose house Spender stayed in May 1927 (*WWW* 33).

Sonnet on Absence

"He took me through his country": Spender describes his host as an unhappy man whose trips into the Breton countryside were complicated by his hay fever: "He sat through meals with tears streaming from his sore, red eyes" (*WWW* 33). Spender's eyes, in turn, are blinded by homesickness and longing for Winifred (who appears as "Caroline" in his memoir): "I lived at this time for the letters discussing books and art which I received from and wrote to Caroline" (*WWW* 33). See Sutherland 66.

He finds the town . . .

". . . a cathedral, and a chateau of old dukes. . .": The Cathedral St. Pierre and the Château des ducs de Bretagne in the center of Nantes. The castle was home to the Dukes of Brittany until the sixteenth century, when the French monarchy appropriated it as their residence in the Bretagne.

The Chateau Garden

"In this old garden . . .": Likely a reference to the moat garden of the Château des ducs de Bretagne.

"And there are artists poets & dandies / Whose narrow wit their only stand is": See also the introduction. Note the clumsy rhyme, illustrative of the difficulty later described by Julian Symons: "one can never be sure with Spender whether or not the comedy is deliberate." Possibly an attempt to slight those who "narrowly" think of literature as amusement.

He does not like the youth of the town . . .

At the Lycée Clemenceau, Spender took a class on the Napoleonic wars in which the teacher apologized to him for disparaging references to the British the historical truth obliged him to make. Meanwhile, the French boys in the classroom, lacking access to more graphic material, were surreptitiously passing around newspaper articles dealing with "women's complaints and menstruation" (*WWW* 34).

Stanzas

The only poem from this volume besides "The Original Bluebeard" to have appeared in print elsewhere. With minor changes in punctuation and the word "harp" substituted for "lyre" in stanza 3, "Stanzas" appeared in *The Beanstalk*, the literary journal published by the University College School Literary Society, in June 1927, which raises the possibility that Spender mailed it from France.

I

"sickneth": Likely an error for "sickeneth."

III

". . . a lyre divinelier strung / Than Virgil's . . .": The "enchanting lyre" of Orpheus is mentioned in Virgil's *Aeneid*, Book VI (trans. John Dryden). In Book I, Satire X, Horace lists the genres with which his satires compete, among them the pastoral, the product of the "graceful tenderness of Virgil's lyre" (trans. David Hunter). Finally, in Swinburne's dramatic monologue "Anactoria" (1866), the poet Sappho refers to her lover's body as "a lyre of many faultless agonies" upon which she plays, an instrument that inflicts pain even as it produces pleasurable sounds.

There are roses in his hosts' garden . . .

George Puttenham, in *The Arte of English Poesy* (1589), defines as the subject of poetry "whatsoever witty and delicate conceit of man worthy or meet to be written in verse," a phrase echoed by Spender's "delicate conceit." But rather than linger on such older definitions, Spender insists that his "cast of thought" is "objective" and "critical" rather than "personal," which shows him to be an attentive reader of Eliot's essays, notably "Tradition and the Individual Talent" (1919) and "The Metaphysical Poets" (1921).

She Holds a Rose

The intended spacing of this poem is not entirely clear; the transcription given here assumes that the poem's last and first lines serve as a frame for the indented main part of the poem.

The plucked rose as a metaphor for the sexual act is stock in trade, but Spender's persona poem varies the tradition by having a woman's fingers be the agents of the potential destruction. Rimbaud's satirical sketch "Un cœur sous une soutane" (posthumously published in 1924, first in Breton's magazine *Littérature* and then in book form, with prefaces by André Breton and Louis Aragon) features a young, sensually deprived seminarian in love with a girl named Thimothima. He plucks the strings of his lyre like the petals of a rose: "Oh! si vous saviez les effluves mystérieux qui secouaient mon âme pendant que j'effeuillais cette rose poétique.

Je pris ma cithare, et comme le psalmiste, j'élevai ma voix innocente et pure dans les célestes altitudes!!!" (Oh! if you knew the mysterious effluvia which shook my soul while I plucked the petals of this poetic rose! I seized my cithara, and, like the psalmist, I raised my innocent and pure voice into the celestial altitudes!!!; Rimbaud 9). But the speaker's earnestness is mocked when the sacristan's wife, an old crone with black teeth, literally plucks a rose before his eyes.

"O 'tis": A revision of the last line, which originally read: "And 'tis."

He is astounded . . .

Note Spender's excited misspelling of "oppressiveness."

Fragment for a Possible Romance

"apopleptic": Spender's misspelling for "apoplectic."

". . . dart in puzzled cubes": The first poem in the collection to show signs of deliberate revision. Spender's text bursts with anticipation, with sky and landscape thickening into tangibility as a thunderstorm draws near, a tribute perhaps to Eliot's *The Waste Land*, where the promise of healing rain finally dissolves the feverish tension built up throughout the poem. Imagining the flight of the swallows three-dimensionally (as "puzzled cubes"), Spender flattens the image again by describing, in the next two lines, how a bird's cry cuts sound into shapes (as if indeed they were creating puzzle pieces). The surreal mix of concrete sense impressions and abstract generalizations captures well the charged atmosphere that precedes the downpour: a seeking for release that Spender unabashedly sexualizes. A prose equivalent is Austrian writer Stefan Zweig's simmering story "Die Frau und die Landschaft" ("The Woman and the Landscape," 1917). For a similarly spatialized image of birds, see Spender's "In a Garden" (from *Ruins and Visions*, 1942): "the singing of those birds / Pressed to the hot wall of the sky, / Tears through the listening writing of the eye / To a space beyond words" (*NCP* 182).

"But see now!": Written in block letters in Spender's manuscript.

Two Sonnets

See also the note on *"He does not like the youth of the town. . . ."* In "My parents kept me from children who were rough" (*Poems* [1933]), Spender remembers the reasons for his revulsion against, and attraction to, boys not restrained by Victorian codes of behavior: "I feared more than tigers their muscles like iron / And their jerking hands and their knees tight on my arms" (*NCP* 9).

I

"And I called doing what I least could trust. . .": Before Spender's revision the line was somewhat clearer, although the "it" must have seemed confusing: "And charged with doing what it least could trust."

". . . I find all naked form divine": Spender's suppressed novel *The Temple* (originally written in 1929 and published, after revisions by Spender himself, in 1988) evokes his fascination with nude male bodies, so frequently on display during the brief period of sexual permissiveness characteristic of Weimar Germany, where most of the novel is set. Spender's protagonist, Paul, celebrates "these young Germans having a new attitude to the body" and reflects critically on his upbringing: "Although I have never been puritanical in outlook, I confess that till now, whatever I may have pretended to myself, I have always regarded my body as sinful, and my own physical being as something to be ashamed of. . . . Now I am beginning to feel that I may soon come to regard my body as a source of joy. . . . Perhaps, after all, I may become a complete human being" (*T* 54). As one of his new German friends mercilessly observes, looking at Paul's unathletic body: "Too much poetry doesn't improve the flesh, even if it does the spirit" (*T* 56). But too little poetry is detrimental too, as Paul finds out when he sees the sun-warmed bodies of his German friends slip on Nazi uniforms, their muscular arms stiffening in the Nazi salute.

II

"But if it cease to burn . . .": Spender's previous version was "And if it cease to strike . . . ."

"And so I'd fall, because to sin is better / Than be called sinning, doing no such matter": Note the Shakespearean echoes in the sonnets. Spender's revises the original concluding line ("Than be called sinner, being no such matter") to a version more like King Lear's self- characterization: "I am a man / More sinn'd against than sinning" (III.2). He also alludes to the concluding couplet of Sonnet 87: "Thus have I had thee, as a dream doth flatter, / In sleep a king, but waking no such matter." The note added in blue ink clarifies the revision.

The Confession of the Monk Struck Blind by Lightening [*sic*]

According to Spender's own note, this was one of the most worked-over entries in the collection. Lustful monks are a staple in world literature, from Boccaccio's *Decamerone* to Matthew Lewis's *The Monk* to Charles Baudelaire's "Mauvais Moine" (Bad Monk) from *Fleurs du Mal* (1857). Occasionally, monks are stricken with blindness, as a punishment for past transgressions (Count Hugo, for example, in Longfellow's *The Golden Legend*). Spender's narrative is also reminiscent of the blinding of Saul/St. Paul in Acts 9:3–9 and perhaps also of the 1902 rape of the 11-year-old Italian girl Maria Goretti by a neighbor who subsequently became a Capuchin lay brother, but since Goretti wasn't beatified before 1947 (and canonized in 1950), it is unlikely that Spender knew the story.

Beginning with this poem, Spender numbers his pages—first in pencil, then in ink.

3

"In drunken living wost the night and day . . .": Probably archaic for "wasted." Spender shows his erudition by using the Middle English form.

8

"Received her beauty's thief & nought did say . . .": Originally, Spender had written "her beauty's gift."

11

"Glanced forth Molania . . .": A new goddess Spender created. Note the mix of Pagan and Christian symbolism in the poem.

13

"and many-wheres . . .": A rare adverb, in line with other archaisms in this poem. See the translation of Psalm 107 by Mary Herbert, Countess of Pembroke (c. 1595): "How many whers doth he convert / Well watred grounds to thirsty sand?"

"A vague acute-edged cry . . .": Spender recycles a metaphor from "Fragment for a Possible Romance."

16

"her's to avenge . . .": Note Spender's unconventional (and ungrammatical) use of the apostrophe with possessive pronouns here and elsewhere in this stanza ("her's"; "your's").

Song

"Though the poet be gone": Spender's version of a pervasive theme in Shakespeare's sonnets, as in 19 ("My love shall in my verse ever live young") and 55 ("Not marble nor the gilded monuments / Of princes shall outlive this pow'rful rhyme").

To a Poet

A generalized appeal to an unspecified and yet undiscovered "stronger" poet-mentor, a role W. H. Auden would assume a year later in Spender's life (Sutherland 78).

"Than mine (unnurtured), for it needs such might": Note the original version of the line, before the strikeouts: "Than mine being gold, and worthy of [valuing] such might." The revision places the emphasis on the stronger poet's requested intervention, away from the question of how deserving the speaker is.

"Posessing": Spender's misspelling.

The Boy Who Was Called "The Nightingale"

Perhaps the first openly homoerotic poem in the collection. The nightingale as a figure for the poet (Philomela, in Greek myth) has a long, distinguished history, culminating in poems such as John Keats's "Ode to a Nightingale" or Samuel Taylor Coleridge's "To a Nightingale." Traditionally construed as female, the bird here appears masculinized. The boy is also addressed as a "hyacinth," a reference to Apollo's beautiful boy lover-turned-plant, and as a lily, which in Greek myth has both feminine and masculine connotations. Said to have sprung from drops of Hera's breastmilk, the lily acquired its phallic-looking pistils later, at the jealous Aphrodite's request, as a blemish visited on its pristine beauty. Spender also recalls Sonnet 102, where Shakespeare compares his poetry to the nightingale's song and promises that, like her, he will sometimes be silent so as not to "dull" his male lover with his song.

Gender ambiguities abound in the poem's first part (note the nightingale boy's fairy voice, white throat, and softly feathered belly). In the second part, all of nature appears to rush in to feast on the boy's cherry lips. The deletion before the title indicates that Spender at first intended to add "The Original Bluebeard" here (see p. 62) and then changed his mind—proof that he had planned the arrangement of poems in the manuscript.

To illustrate the genesis of this poem, I have in this one instance changed the sequence of manuscript pages, since Spender completed his poem on the verso of the page preceding the poem's last page. The discarded passage, with previous deletions restored in square brackets reads:

> And all things were [the] accompaniment
> [Became of that sweet] [Were] To his sweet voice, the instrument
> And to those swift violins this song
> From his blythe heart today was sung:—

Spender then adds and crosses out the text of a poem used earlier in the collection, "Song."

A

2

"We will throw violets, roses, speedwell . . ." Speedwell is a tough perennial also known as the Veronica (other names are "bird's eye" or "gypsyweed").

3

"The faery voice . . .": Spender had originally begun writing another adjective, possibly "perfumed."

5

"Like those bewildered weathers": Perhaps a reference to Book X of Homer's *Odyssey*, where Odysseus' men secretly open the bag given to them by Aeolus, releasing the storms that blow them back to Aeolus's island and thus prolong their voyage.

B

I have moved the date, originally given after the discarded passage, to the end of part B.

"Played subtly in his woried [*sic*] brain . . .": Spender's misspelling.

The Original Bluebeard, Gilles de Rais of Brittany

Buried close to where Spender had lived in Nantes, Gilles de Montmorency-Laval, Baron de Rais (1405–1440) was a confessed serial killer of, possibly, hundreds of children. The poem derives its effectiveness from its focus on the repeated rhyme, created by enjambment: "Rais'/face." This was the only poem from *Poems Written Abroad* to be included in Spender's *Nine Experiments*, a collection of poems Spender typeset himself in 1928. Titled "Gilles," the poem is essentially the same, apart from some adventurous use of spacing and capitalization. The wobbly typeface, the missing closing quote in the final line of the poem, and the italicized "h" in "right" only add to the homemade charm of the collection:

> And turned rig*h*t round and said:—
> 'O Gilles de Rais' FACE *AND*
>   BEARD!
> (*Nine Experiments* 16)

Written after the Fête de Dieu

Impressed—apparently none too favorably—by a Catholic procession he witnessed in Nantes, Spender, in this Petrarchan sonnet, makes a show of renouncing meat, likening this type of animal sacrifice to forms of Christian martyrdom.

"And finding there the same, my heart shall turn . . .": Original version: "I shall remember, and my heart shall turn."

"And martyrs over great fires made to burn . . .": Originally: "And Christians over great fires"

"Christ's great heart broke . . .": The "ruptured heart" hypothesis was first proposed in 1847 by the Scottish physician William Stroud, in *The Physical Cause of the Death of Christ*.

A Sonnet to Be Beautifully Printed at the Beginning of His Poems

Another Petrarchan sonnet, not perfectly structured, since it has technically two *volte* (after "lay" and "rhythm"). The birth of a poem is likened to the emergence of a new star on the "purpurean" firmament. The self-conscious literariness of Spender's writing is somewhat offset by the intensity of the color scheme he creates: the milky moon bathing in white, the wine-tinged sky over hills that, in the darkness, look like slumbering sheep. The autograph shows evidence of minor revision throughout, such as in the emendation of "Were fat as sheep" to "As white as sheep," a change that reflects Spender's pervasive interest in visual effects. Readers will be grateful for the substitution of the adjective "youngest" for "baby" in the poem's last line ("Do you not see my new, my youngest star?").

"Cleft black bettween . . .": Spender's misspelling.

After Ronsard

The first evidence of Spender's talents as a translator. Pierre de Ronsard's sonnet "Sur la mort de Marie" was written in 1574 on behalf of the duke of Anjou (the future Henri III), whose mistress Marie de Clèves had just died (Ronsard, *Selected Poems* 39). The poem might have resonated with Spender because of the centrality of the rose metaphor but also because of Ronsard's evident poetic skill in handling a relatively contrite theme while staying entirely within the allusive conventions of Renaissance poetry:

> Comme on voit sur la branche au mois de May la rose,
> En sa belle jeunesse, en sa premiere fleur,
> Rendre le ciel jaloux de sa vive couleur,
> Quand l'aube de ses pleurs au poinct du jour l'arrose:
>
> La grace dans sa feuille, et l'amour se repose,
> Embasmant les jardins et les arbres d'odeur;
> Mais battue ou de pluye ou d'excessive ardeur,
> Languissante elle meurt feuille à feuille déclose.
>
> Ainsi en ta premiere et jeune nouveauté,
> Quand la terre et le ciel honoroient ta beauté,
> La Parque t'a tuée, et cendre tu reposes.
>
> Pour obseques reçoy mes larmes et mes pleurs,
> Ce vase plein de laict, ce pannier plein de fleurs,
> Afin que vif et mort ton corps ne soit que roses.
> (*The Oxford Book of French Verse* 55)

Spender follows the original closely where he can, as in the poem's first line, where Ronsard purposely delays mention of the rose to the end, as if wanting to imitate the way "the rose seems to sway gently at the extremity of a flexible stem" (Odette de Morgue, "Ronsard's Later Poetry" 291). But he also feels free to change Ronsard's original when necessary, especially in the last triplet of the sestet, where he restores agency to the mistress, asking her to "take these tears of ours" instead of, literally, to "receive my tears." Note also how closely he follows Ronsard's rhyme scheme, in the final three lines even approximating the sounds ("-eurs; -eurs; -oses" and "ours; -owers; -oses"). In the preface to his translation of Rilke's *The Life of the Virgin Mary* (1951), Spender would describe translation as the result of compromise, of using one's own resources as a poet to "hint at rather than attempt to give the original" (9).

Tail-Piece

In music, a tailpiece is the part of a string instrument that anchors the strings, as opposed to the pegs, where the strings end. The term can also refer to a decorative element added at the end of a chapter or book. It is possible that Spender, knowing that he would leave Nantes soon, was trying to find a suitable ending for his manuscript. The musical allusion and the form of the prose poem, complete with ecstatic exclamations, reveal the influence of Rimbaud.

The Ballad of Money

The first poem definitively written after Spender's arrival in Lausanne, Switzerland. Residing in an expensive "pension," where he enjoyed his own room with balcony and mountain views, Spender promptly fell in love with another boarder, an English boy named David Maclean. Spender describes his infatuation in a story he wrote at time, "By the Lake," his "first significant work in prose," according to John Sutherland (70). It was later published in *The Burning Cactus*. In this story, "Richard" (Spender's alias) freely confesses his desire for "Donauld" (Maclean), attributing his homosexuality to self-experimentation in school, when, for lack of alternatives, his feverish mind attached itself to male bodies. Donauld balks, appalled less by Richard's advances than by his atheism.

3

"beauty that I shall never know": The sight of Lake Geneva engenders a reflection on places (far east and far north) the poet thinks he will never see and on experiences he hasn't had. The poem travels backward and then forward in western history, moving from ancient Rome, Egypt, and Greece (a homosexual paradise where men went their "married way") to the voyages of Sir Francis Drake and Sir Walter Raleigh's hunt for El Dorado. Spender then shifts to the present and criticizes the adoration of money that has replaced the earlier spirit of adventure. The last stanza links this loss of innocence somewhat awkwardly to man's fall from Grace in the Garden of Eden.

9

"The men whom man has conquered": Spender's handwriting is ambiguous. While "man" would make more sense grammatically, I have opted for the more poetically persuasive "men."

11

"O is he not too beautiful . . .": In its original form, the line read: "O is not Man too beautiful."

Clair de Lune

Claude Debussy's "Clair de Lune," the third movement of his *Suite bergamasque* (published 1905), was inspired by Paul Verlaine's 1865 poem "Clair de Lune," a fanciful description of the soul as a landscape across which masked, unhappy clowns dance. They sing in a minor key ("sur le mode mineur"), and their sad songs mingle with the moonlight as birds dream in the trees and fountains sob in ecstasy (Verlaine 28). Spender populates *his* surreal landscape—inspired by the "alpenglow" over the mountains he could have seen from his balcony—with actual composers, from Bach ("John Sebastian") to Beethoven to Igor Stravinsky. (For more on this poem, see the introduction to this volume).

The fact that Beethoven composed his most enduring pieces as he was facing permanent deafness remained powerfully interesting to Spender, perhaps because he knew that they were, artistically, polar opposites. Whereas Spender depended on external influences for inspiration, Beethoven found enough inside himself to compose works of enduring influence. Beethoven, Spender wrote, "was able to use as material for his music the discordant noises he heard in his ears instead of hearing." Beethoven's late quartets especially captivated Spender, since they offered glimpses of "a distant, blue range of mountains beyond a rolling desert" (see Spender's journal entries for November 30, 1932 and October 22, 1939, in *Letters to Christopher* 156, 199–200). Among Spender's Beethoven poems are "Beethoven's Death Mask" (in *Poems* [1933], *NCP* 7, and "Late Stravinsky Listening to Late Beethoven" (1972/1985; *NCP* 323–24).

It is not clear if the curved line through much of the first half of the poem indicates that Spender wanted that section excised. There are other minor revisions: "the Madrigal / That stirs" becomes "a Madrigal / Stirring," and "Mozart plays so fast" is reduced to "Mozart plays." Spender makes an effort to resist his own inclination towards prolixity.

"heart-apaling": Spender's misspelling.

To W. E. P.

Alarmed by Stephen's entanglements, Winifred Paine had sent Spender a letter to inform him that "she was gravely ill and must have an operation." Seized by guilt because of his infatuation with David Maclean, he felt the need to return home immediately: "I suffered for her and was torn with anxiety." When he arrived in London, Winifred had recovered (*WWW* 35). Minor revisions lend a more physical note to the poem: "And stifled the maiden Day" becomes "And choked the maiden Day," and Spender enhances the contrast he aims for when he evokes the "swift" (rather than originally just "fresh") "waters" that stiffen under the impact of his friend's illness.

Consolation of Dust

3

"Love, virtue, light . . .": Originally, "Woman, and light . . ."

"Oh earth of beauty . . .": Originally, "Oh changling beauty . . ."

4

"But in thy dazed and self-reflective ease . . .": Originally, "But in thy dazed and self-reflected love."

"Thou still must hear a Dust beneath thy sod . . .": A rather surprising allusion to a popular song from the American Civil War. "Lorena" (1857), written by the Reverend Henry D. L. Webster, after a broken engagement, and set by Joseph Philbrick Webster, offers a tribute to a girl from Zanesville, Ohio, who was forced to marry someone other than the distraught lyricist. The song ends with the comforting thought that what remains separate on earth and in death will be united in heaven: "'Tis dust to dust beneath the sod / But there, up there, 'tis heart to heart." By contrast, Spender's elusive lover is beauty incarnate and her demands will, he fears, survive the poet's death.

BIBLIOGRAPHY

For titles by Stephen Spender quoted throughout, see the List of Abbreviations.

Auden, W. H. *Collected Shorter Poems 1927–1957.* 1966. London: Faber and Faber, 1969.
Beethoven, Ludwig van. *Briefe Beethovens.* Ed. Hugo Leichtentritt. Berlin: Deutsche Bibliothek [1912].
David, Hugh. *Stephen Spender: A Portrait with Background.* London: Heinemann, 1992.
Eliot, T. S. *Selected Prose of T. S. Eliot.* Ed. Frank Kermode. London: Faber and Faber, 1975.
Hitchens, Christopher. *Arguably: Essays by Christopher Hitchens.* Toronto: Signal, 2011.
Kulkarni, H. B. *Stephen Spender, Works and Criticism: An Annotated Bibliography.* New York: Garland, 1976.
Leeming, David. *Stephen Spender: A Life in Modernism.* New York: Henry Holt, 1999.
Metcalf, Stephen. "Stephen Spender, Toady: Was There Any Substance to His Politics and Art?," *Slate*, February 7, 2005, http://www.slate.com/articles/arts/books/2005/02/stephen_spender_toady.html
Morgues, Odette de. "Ronsard's Later Poetry." In *Ronsard the Poet*, edited by Terence Cave, 287–31. London: Methuen, 1973.
O'Hagan, Andrew. "From Soup to Fish." *London Review of Books* (December 17, 2015): 9–10.
The Oxford Book of French Verse, 13th Century–19th Century. Ed. John Lucas. Oxford: Clarendon, 1908.
Rilke, Rainer Maria. *The Life of the Virgin Mary.* Translated by Stephen Spender. New York: Philosophical Library, 1951.
Rimbaud, Arthur. *Un cœur sous une soutane: Intimités d'un séminariste.* Paris: Ronald Davis, 1924.
Ronsard, Pierre de. *Selected Poems.* Edited Malcolm Quainton and Elizabeth Vinestock. London: Penguin, 2002.
Sansom, Ian. "Too Busy with Other Things," *The Guardian*, June 12, 2004, https://www.theguardian.com/books/2004/jun/12/featuresreviews.guardianreview16.
Spender, Matthew. *A House in St John's Wood: In Search of My Parents.* New York: Farrar, Straus and Giroux, 2015.
Spender, Stephen. *The Backward Son.* London: Hogarth, 1940.
———. *The Creative Element: A Study of Vision, Despair and Orthodoxy among Some Modern Writers.* London: Hamish Hamilton, 1953.

——. *Letters to Christopher: Stephen Spender's Letters to Christopher Isherwood 1929–1939.* Ed. Lee Bartlett. Santa Barbara: Black Sparrow Press, 1980.

——. *Love-Hate Relations: A Study of Anglo-American Sensibilities.* London: Hamish Hamilton, 1974.

——. *Nine Experiments by S.H.S.: Being Poems Written at the Age of Eighteen.* Privately printed, 1928. Facsimile. Cincinnati, Ohio: Elliston Poetry Foundation, 1964.

——. "Stanzas." *The Beanstalk* 1.4 (June, 1927): 103–104.

——. *The Struggle of the Modern.* Berkeley: University of California Press, 1963.

Sutherland, John. *Stephen Spender: The Authorized Biography.* 2004. London: Penguin, 2005.

Symons, Julian. "A Self-Lacerating Frankness." *Times Literary Supplement*, February 18, 1994.

Vendler, Helen. *The Music of What Happens: Poems, Poets, Critics.* Cambridge, MA: Harvard University Press, 1988.

——. *The Art of Shakespeare's Sonnets.* Cambridge, MA: Belknap, 1997.

Verlaine, Paul. *One Hundred and One Poems by Paul Verlaine: A Bilingual Edition.* Translated by Norman R. Shapiro. Chicago: University of Chicago Press, 1999.

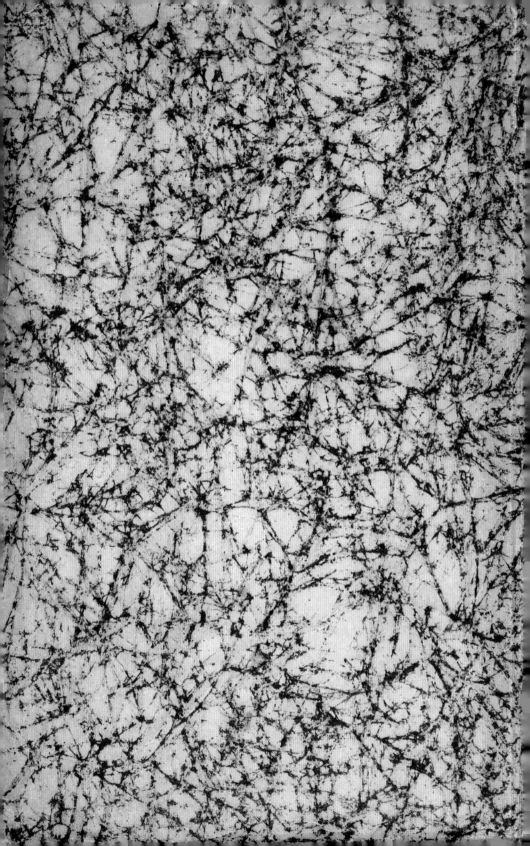

CHRISTOPH IRMSCHER is Provost Professor of English and Director of the Wells Scholars Program at Indiana University. His many books include *Louis Agassiz: Creator of American Science* and *Max Eastman: A Life*.

GARY DUNHAM	Director
PEGGY SOLIC	Acquisitions Editor
ANNA FRANCIS	Project Manager
JENNIFER WITZKE	Cover Designer
TONY BREWER	Layout & Composition